I know Debbie and LOVE her books! She's a street-smart genius! Dreams do come true and success really can become easy when you take the right action. Start now by reading this powerful new book!

—Dr. Joe Vitale, author of *Attract Money Now* and *Zero Limits*

If you are ready for more sⸯⸯⸯⸯ t in your life, *Success Is Easy* is ⸯⸯⸯⸯ ⸯcome your go-to guide for yeⸯ ⸯⸯⸯⸯ gets of how-to ⸯⸯ

—T. Harv Eker, N. ⸯⸯbestselling author of *Secrets of ⸯⸯ Millionaire Mind*™

Success Is Easy is a practical, powerful, and inspiring book for anyone who is ready to shift to a new level of fulfillment and mastery in business. Debbie Allen has written an important and insightful guide containing many treasures of advice and wisdom to help you create the success you deserve.

—Dr. Barbara De Angelis, *New York Times* bestselling author and transformational teacher

If you are ready to WIN in business despite any obstacle, you must read *Success Is Easy*! This brilliant book is your action guide to finally start achieving success the easy way!

—Greg Reid, author of *Wealth Made Easy*

You are about to step into the shoes of someone who has proven that success is attainable. Debbie Allen has utilized the exact concepts she shares with you to achieve multiple successes. That's the test of a proven formula. Is it repeatable? The answer is YES! Be prepared to elevate your success exponentially by implementing Debbie's practical and powerful wisdom.

—Glenna Salsbury, CSP, CPAE, Speaker Hall of Fame and author of *The Art of the Fresh Start*

Success Is Easy is a life-changing book that can inspire anyone to achieve more success and confidence in their life with ease!

—RUBEN GONZALEZ, OLYMPIAN, SPEAKER, AND AUTHOR

Debbie Allen's must-read book *Success Is Easy* is for anyone who feels challenged when achieving success. This book will turn your head to a new way of thinking, believing, doing, and achieving by creating a success-driving mindset.

—JOHN SPENCER ELLIS, HOST OF *THE ENTREPRENEUR SHOW*

If you want unlimited success, more money, and the mindset to overcome any obstacle, *Success Is Easy* is a MUST READ! Over the 30-plus years I have known Debbie Allen, I've seen her turn obstacles into opportunities time and time again. With her no-nonsense success strategies you will become unstoppable too!

—JOEL WELDON, SPEAKER HALL OF FAME

If you change the way you think about success, it can become easy. Debbie Allen's latest book *Success is Easy* will show you how to make the shifts you need for your own unique version of success, and guide you on your path towards a much higher level of success for life!

—CHRISTY WHITMAN, *NEW YORK TIMES* BESTSELLING AUTHOR

Once again, Debbie Allen has broken down the mindset and action steps it takes to achieve true success—as you define it. Debunking traditional and outdated wisdom, she shines the light on how success can actually be EASY when you have the right approach. A must-read for any leader, entrepreneur, or professional who wants to succeed in life and business!

—MARCIA BENCH, CEO OF CONSCIOUS EXPERTS ACADEMY
AND 26-TIME AUTHOR

Success Is Easy will change the way you think about success forever! Debbie Allen pulls back the curtain to reveal the secrets to achieving lasting success with ease from her decades of business building success. She will teach you about obtaining success with her get-to-the point style and shameless secrets to achieving much more by climbing over obstacles with ease. This book is a must read for anyone wanting serious success.

—LEE MILTEER, BUSINESS AND LIFE STRATEGIST

A unique voice on success that every entrepreneur needs to read! You'll never let limiting thoughts, habits, or actions stop you again.

—KENDALL SUMMERHAWK, LEADER OF THE #1 CERTIFIED COACH TRAINING FOR WOMEN ENTREPRENEURS

It shocks most people to learn that success is easy, simple, and attainable if you know the secrets. We succeed more based upon what we know than how hard we work. Therefore, it should be our lifelong quest to learn success lessons. In this book, Debbie Allen offers real, practical, and time-tested methods to succeed.

—JIM STOVALL, AUTHOR OF THE ULTIMATE GIFT

I can't think of anyone better to write a book about success than someone who has achieved it time and time again as a self-made entrepreneur since a young age. In Debbie Allen's latest book *Success Is Easy*, she explores how to think bigger, develop passion and commitment, overcome the fear of failure, and avoid acceptance of false beliefs. Debbie shatters myths and explains that success is easier than failure and is achievable at any age!

—DR. DIANE HAMILTON, CEO AND FOUNDER OF TONERRA AND AUTHOR OF *CRACKING THE CURIOSITY CODE*

What do you believe about success? I have a hunch you picked up this book because you still feel a little (or a lot) stuck in your business. Well, congratulations on choosing a book and an author who will powerfully help you shift your limiting beliefs about what success really means and how you can have it NOW. I've known Debbie Allen for years and she has a no-nonsense way of breaking down barriers and showing her clients, and her readers, how they can pave their path to success on their own terms. Get ready to debunk the success myths and decide now to make it easy!

—URSULA MENTJES, AWARD-WINNING AUTHOR, ENTREPRENEUR, AND SALES EXPERT

Debbie Allen has done it again! She has figured out how to take everything that has made her successful and transform that into a masterpiece that will prove to you that *Success Is Easy*. And the good news is that not only is success easy, but this read is easy, too. It's the kind of book you'll read quickly—because you'll want to read it again. Success is easy—and the decision to buy this book is easy!

—DAVID GLICKMAN, SPEAKER HALL OF FAME AND AUTHOR OF
SPEAKING OF FUNNY

Success Is Easy will change the way you think about success forever! Debbie Allen pulls back the curtain to reveal the secrets to achieving lasting success with ease from her decades of business building success.

— LISA SASEVICH, THE QUEEN OF SALES CONVERSION

success
is easy

SHAMELESS
NO-NONSENSE
STRATEGIES TO WIN
IN BUSINESS

Debbie Allen

Entrepreneur Press®

Entrepreneur Press, Publisher
Cover Design: Andrew Welyczko
Production and Composition: Eliot House Productions

This publication is designed to provide accurate and authoritative information
in regard to the subject matter covered. It is sold with the understanding that
the publisher is not engaged in rendering legal, accounting, or other professional
services. If legal advice or other expert assistance is required, the services of a
competent professional person should be sought.

Entrepreneur Press® is a registered trademark of Entrepreneur Media, Inc.

Library of Congress Cataloging-in-Publication Data
Names: Allen, Debbie, 1953- author.
Title: Success is easy : shameless, no-nonsense strategies to win in business /
     by Debbie Allen.
Description: Irvine, Calif. : Entrepreneur Press, [2019]
Identifiers: LCCN 2019019963| ISBN 978-1-59918-647-4 (alk. paper) |
     ISBN 1-59918-647-0 (alk. paper)
Subjects: LCSH: Success in business. | Strategic planning.
Classification: LCC HF5386 .A5285 2019 | DDC 658.4/09—dc23
LC record available at https://lccn.loc.gov/2019019963

Printed in the United States of America

23 22 21 20 19   10 9 8 7 6 5 4 3 2 1

contents

PART I

REALITY-STRETCHING SUCCESS SECRETS

CHAPTER 1

PART II

SHAMELESS SELF-PROMOTION AND STRATEGIC MARKETING

CHAPTER 5

CHAPTER 6

CHAPTER 7

PART III

PROVEN SUCCESS PRINCIPLES TO WIN IN BUSINESS

PART IV

COMITMENT TO EXCELLENCE AND GROWTH

CHAPTER 14

CHAPTER 15

CHAPTER 16

CHAPTER 17

PART V
STEPPING UP TO A HIGHER LEVEL OF SUCCESS

foreword
by Jeffrey Hayzlett

*Primetime TV and podcast host, bestselling author
of* Think Big, Act Bigger *(Entrepreneur Press, 2015)
and* The Hero Factor *(Entrepreneur Press, 2018),
and part-time cowboy*

Debbie Allen's *Success Is Easy* offers a fresh, no-nonsense approach to empowering readers who are beginning their journey toward success. This book also covers the critical business concepts to support already-successful entrepreneurs who want to dive deeper and grow their business to the next level.

The principles in this book provide a forward-thinking mindset and teach common business sense that's not found anywhere else. The thought-provoking ideas, tips, case studies, and proven business strategies will lift businesspeople out of their rut and put them on the right path to success, whatever their definition of success is.

Whether you're gun-shy by nature or feel stuck in your current situation, this book will help you visualize and manage the bold action steps required to move ahead and win in business.

I suggest reading this book from cover to cover. Turn to any page and gain instant knowledge in areas you need to focus on most right now. Keep this book in a personal success library as a reference and share it with business associates.

Saddle up! And dare to be honest while you read through this book and consider what you need to change and improve in your life. That's how to gain the most insight from this book, and your success journey will become easier, with fewer bumps and obstacles along the way. And who knows what you might actually discover in this pot of gold on the other side?

introduction

Do you really need another book on success? Thousands of books on success and goal setting already sit on bookshelves around the world. But what is missing in those books is a real-world, say-it-like-it-is focus on no-nonsense, proven principles and shameless strategies for achieving success. There is a huge gap of practical advice, which is probably why most people still think of success as hard—or even unattainable. This mindset is instilled in them at a very young age. But it is simply not true!

If I believed success was hard, I would have failed or struggled with money my entire life. I got poor grades in school and barely graduated from high school. I never attended a day of college in my life. I never even applied for a job. According to popular belief, with my background, I was destined to be broke or at best live paycheck to paycheck just to survive. But some how I built and sold multiple million-dollar companies in diverse industries, beginning at the young age of 19.

I succeeded many more times than I failed, simply because I believed in winning. My goal is to achieve success—to do whatever it takes to never have to work for anyone else for the rest of my life.

I am an independent thinker and know how to break the rules. Much of what I learned in business was taught in the proverbial school of hard knocks. I believe I can be successful at anything I set my mind to, even when I am clueless about how to do something.

There is nothing special about the way I think about business, except for the fact that I always believe I can succeed, because *Success Is Easy.*

Here's the good news: You don't have to know how to succeed to be successful. Success is taught in almost any business venture. With clarity, focus, and commitment, you can easily learn proven business skills from already successful people to gain the knowledge you need to build, grow, and prosper in business.

Taking action is critically important for achieving success, but those actions will fail until you master the deeply personal aspects driving success. The hard truth is that success isn't just a series of actions. It is an attitude, a belief, and a hard-wired commitment.

Discover That Success Is Not Just Possible—It's Easy!

Success Is Easy is a guide to what is possible. It pulls no punches in unveiling the truth about how easy it is to build a successful business. This book is designed to demystify success by introducing reality-stretching principles that work in any type of business.

Success Is Easy presents a no-excuses approach to turning timid, fearful, unclear, or stuck businesspeople into fearless, shameless, and powerful influencers who are willing to do whatever it takes to achieve success.

This empowering book encourages those who have failed in the past to step up and become winners. It will help turn negative complainers into positive, abundant stewards of success!

The key points in this book encourage you to visualize your own success, to pay close attention to the amazing opportunities surrounding you every day, and to know when to say "no" to opportunities that don't serve and support your goals. The thought-provoking, reality-gripping ideas, case studies, and business strategies I share will inspire you not just to take action, but to jump into bold, shameless action. And to do that, there are a few tips you should keep in mind as you read the book. Let's walk through them.

Success Is Defined Differently for Every Person

First, remember that success is defined differently for each person at different times in life. You are asked to define your own success in great detail so you can begin to feel it. This allows a deeper understanding of your "what" and "why" to give meaning and a sense of accomplishment once you arrive at success. Then it's a matter of learning how to set a new benchmark to keep rising to a higher level.

Success Is a Road Paved with Obstacles and Opportunities

Although you can have an easy road to success, your journey will generally be paved with hurdles and obstacles to test you along the way. True desires and commitments are tested so you can learn lessons, improve, grow, and feel the satisfaction of achieving your goals. Think about that for a moment. *Have you overcome challenges? Once you overcame an obstacle, did you learn a lesson?* And, most important, *Did it give you a feeling of satisfaction and achievement? Did it make you feel more confident and more successful?*

Most obstacles are caused by negative beliefs that may not even be true. The obstacles may only be perceived or assumed, but once they stick in your mind, they may appear insurmountable.

A destructive mindset will block, limit, sabotage, and often destroy your chances for success. You may discover that crushing any limiting beliefs will lead to seeing more success show up everywhere, almost like magic. Why? Because looking at the opportunities that surround you every day with a more positive mindset allows you to see a new world of limitless success.

For example, in business, it really isn't a question of if something will go wrong. Rather, it's a matter of when: *How do you respond, make adjustments, and move forward?* That is what will determine your level of success.

The only thing that can turn mistakes into failures is when a person does not learn from the mistakes. Lessons are gifts of success in disguise. They are given to you to expand your thinking and to offer you a challenge for positive change.

The common-sense business advice and shameless strategies in this book will challenge you to roll up your sleeves and get to work when mistakes or obstacles appear—but only if you are serious about wanting more success in your business and your life.

How to Use This Book

I wrote this book to share my life's work with you. In the process, I've learned to expand my own thinking and beliefs around the concept of success. The goal of this book is to get you fired up to become the best version of yourself. It doesn't matter if your idea of success is running a business, growing a franchise, or becoming a financially independent entrepreneur. This book aims to raise your existing standards and move you toward achieving your limitless success potential.

There is no magic pill for achieving success. But this book will put you on the right path toward accomplishing more with drive and determination and much more success than you currently possess.

Reading *Success Is Easy* strategies and taking action is easy, too. This book provides bite-sized chunks of easy-to-swallow business wisdom that will help you create abundance and success.

The book is divided into five main parts:

- Part I: Reality-Stretching Success Secrets
- Part II: Shameless Self-Promotion and Strategic Marketing
- Part III: Proven Success Principles to Win in Business
- Part IV: Commitment to Excellence and Growth
- Part V: Stepping Up to a Higher Level of Success

You may, of course, read the book cover to cover (and I hope you do!), but also feel free to toggle back and forth between chapters as they apply to your situation. At the end of each chapter, there is a summary with highlights of the chapter to help you stay on track with your goals, with *Shameless, No-Nonsense Action Steps* and a *Success Is Easy Affirmation.*

Let's get started on the road to success right now!

reality-
stretching
success secrets

SUCCESS IS EASY . . .
with a New Reality

Y ou might have been taught that success is challenging. It is hugely disillusioning to grow up and realize that most of what you learned about how to succeed in business is simply bad advice.

In this chapter, you will uncover a new reality about success that you might never have believed possible in the past. You will learn why some people make success look easy. And you will discover why some timeless principles you may have learned about achieving success could backfire on you without a success-driven mindset.

Creating a Success-Driven Mindset

Many of you were told that if you work hard enough, you'll succeed. But that's just not true! Why the hell were you lied to? And why do you still believe it?

Working hard for someone else might get you a paycheck, but there's absolutely no guarantee that it will get you promoted. There is much more to success than simply working hard; if that were the case, millions of people around the world would be a lot more successful!

Hard work doesn't always pay off when you work for yourself, either. I see too many business owners working hard just to tread water, rather than spending their time developing a more successful business.

I know this firsthand. As a new retail store owner, I thought working long hours would help me get ahead. But working harder simply made me more frustrated when success didn't come easily. When I worked harder, I got exhausted and burned out, which made me less productive in growing my business success. Hard work gets things done, but true success also requires innovation, creativity, and new insight.

Too many people believe it's difficult to push through, achieve their goals, and attain all the things they desire. That's completely false.

I should have failed many times in life, but it was my positive mindset and my drive to succeed that pushed me through the most challenging obstacles that stood in my way. In fact, I'm proof that *Success Is Easy* because I:

- started every new business with little or no experience;
- survived despite doomsayers all around telling me I was crazy;
- was a less-than-average student with a very limited education;
- started with very little knowledge of every industry I entered;
- had limited funds for investing into each of my new startups; and
- lost everything a couple of times in my life and started back up from zero to succeed all over again.

Yet despite all these obstacles, success kept finding me again and again.

Why? My passion, determination, and commitment to succeed were stronger than the odds against me. They pushed me to climb over, push down, and tackle any barrier in front of me. I was resolved to move far beyond the norm with a 100 percent commitment to succeed!

Now, I'm not saying you should follow my example of no experience, no knowledge, and no money. You're probably thinking, "That's not a good business model." But it still proves that even with obstacles piling up all around you, you can still succeed with a strong commitment.

It doesn't matter where your drive to succeed comes from; it only matters that you embrace it! I'm not sure where my personal commitment and my passion to succeed come from. No one taught me growing up that this was the way to live your life, but there is something inside me that is independent, shameless, sassy, and strong enough to fight for it. I want more out of life than the status quo, and I know I never want to work for someone else. What do you know about yourself? What do you want?

During the process of success building, you can experience what I have experienced: more happiness, more opportunities, and more money than I ever imagined possible. Once you taste success like this, it gets easier because you have a strong desire to reach your potential.

Win in Business with Belief Shifts

What you learn in this book will lead to winning in business when you apply the following belief shifts:

- You win when you are no longer lost, unclear, or unfocused.
- You succeed by defining what success means to you with a clear vision and a focused path to follow.
- You win by no longer wallowing in self-doubt and worry.
- You succeed with a more positive mindset and belief system.
- You win by no longer needing to blame others for your failures.

- You succeed by turning your mistakes into valuable lessons.
- You win because you stop stressing about your lack of money.
- You succeed by becoming financially free.
- You win by no longer remaining shackled to working hard for someone else and living paycheck to paycheck.
- You succeed because you work smart on your own terms.
- You win because you no longer stress over the competition.
- You succeed because you position yourself to stand out far above the competition.
- You win because you no longer worry about reaching your goals.
- You succeed because you have the courage to take bold, strategic action to achieve your goals every time.
- You win because you are no longer concerned about how to grow and thrive in business.
- You succeed because you continually learn new skills and develop the right traits to level up your knowledge for growth and expansion.
- You win because you no longer allow obstacles and roadblocks to stop you in your tracks.
- You succeed by staying committed to your goals and doing whatever it takes to overcome challenges.
- You win because you no longer fear shameless self-promotion, and you put yourself out there for the world to notice.
- You succeed by learning how to effectively promote yourself and your business in the service of others.
- You win because you make the right decisions quickly and effortlessly.
- You succeed by learning to trust your intuition and your decisions based on past successes.
- You win because you remain open to change and reinvent your business as needed for growth.
- You succeed with each reinvention and understand change is required to expand and grow.
- You win because you are a person of influence.

- You succeed because you are confident and can influence others to follow your ideas and business concepts.
- You win because you do business with integrity and treat others right.
- You succeed by giving others more than expected because you care. This allows you to create an abundance of high-value clients who value your service and refer you to others.

These are the belief shifts you need to make to achieve your own success. And best of all, it can be easy.

Successful People Make It Look Easy

Have you ever wondered how some people succeed almost effortlessly, while others continually fail? First of all, successful people think bigger by raising the bar higher and refusing to accept low standards. Successful people also have a high internal drive to succeed, which allows them to remain persistent.

You could call that drive to succeed *ambition*. Yet if ambition is the key to success, you might also ask, "What drives someone to become more ambitious?"

Is ambition something you can learn or is it something you're born with? I believe anyone can learn to become more ambitious if they want success badly enough to move beyond where they currently are to a better place. They must desire change enough to create an internal drive that moves them to become more ambitious, more passionate, and more motivated by true desires.

So what's the difference?

Successful people make it look effortless because their internal drive keeps them in motion. They don't give up despite obstacles, challenges, and setbacks.

What keeps them going is their ambition. Ambition, or the desire to achieve or succeed in a goal, is a priceless characteristic. Successful people are often described as ambitious. They tend to attract attention in the right areas and get the very best out of life at every turn. Ambition is a positive state of being. It can help you escape obstacles and overcome negative thoughts, which create emotional barriers such as doubt and fear. However, positive thoughts motivate you to move forward and experiment with something new, to step out of your comfort zone, and to get you excited about what lies ahead. And best of all, ambition is something you can create within yourself. You can use it as the fuel to drive success in anything you wish.

To become more ambitious, you need to allow yourself the opportunity to explore and experiment with many new options at once. Success could be waiting right around the corner if you simply look for it.

All you need to develop ambition is consistent drive. Therefore, find out what risks you can take to achieve more success. After that, find out what fear is holding you back from going for it. Once you do this, you create more drive within yourself and begin to face your fear head-on. This will help you become more ambitious toward your goals.

When you allow your ambition level to remain consistent, you stay committed. Commitment is the stubborn willingness to stick to a particular beneficial activity no matter what. Successful people are willing to do whatever it takes, although their commitment can be painful at the beginning when conditions are challenging. However, they understand that focusing on commitment is essential to maintaining their ambition. This may require you to ask yourself what you are willing to give up now to achieve what you want most in the future. It may require a strict schedule to help you stay committed to achieving more. But this kind of commitment will keep you motivated until you begin to achieve success with ease.

We see successful people as winners who make work seem easy. They have mastered their professions. They are confident, focused, ambitious, and committed.

That said, what looks easy is the result of ongoing dedication to success. There is no one secret recipe to becoming a successful person, but there is a list of seven strengths and habits that, when combined, can greatly increase your chances of success.

Seven Strengths and Habits That Successful People Possess

Finding and developing success within yourself can come easily when you look at the strengths and habits of other successful people. The attributes of successful people do not develop overnight and didn't just happen by accident—although they may make it look effortless.

Successful people continue to work on their success habits as part of a daily routine so that success becomes a way of life. Let's walk through seven of the most important strengths and habits of successful people.

1. They Have a Success-Driven Mindset and the Passion to Achieve

Successful people have a strong will to succeed and achieve in life. They look forward to growth and have a deeply rooted desire to do much more than the average person. These people take action to make positive changes and move outside their comfort zone. Even when their attempts fail, they can quickly see opportunities that surround them, adjust when things go wrong, and move in a new direction.

Unsuccessful people, on the other hand, feel defeated, throw their hands up in the air, and give up too soon.

2. They Are Self-Aware and Have Self-Confidence

Successful people face challenges with confidence and trust their skills and knowledge. Even when they don't have the right skills or knowledge to begin with, they move forward with enthusiasm and commitment to succeed despite the odds. Successful people have a strong sense of self, which allows them to make stronger commitments. They are comfortable speaking their minds. Successful people stand up, speak out, and enjoy sharing ideas and opinions.

Unsuccessful people who lack confidence are often unwilling to open up and speak up, which holds them back and causes missed opportunities.

3. They Are Vision-Focused and Achievement-Oriented

Successful people create a clear vision for goals and take action toward achieving that vision, which does not allow anything to stand in their way. A strong vision serves as a guideline to keep them motivated and on track to achieving their goals. They set and conquer smaller goals first and then move on to bigger and bolder benchmarks so they can hit larger targets.

Unsuccessful people are frequently unclear, unfocused, and misguided, so they often waste time and money getting to goals or even missing the targets altogether.

4. They Value Time Wisely

Successful people are extremely productive. They value and use their time wisely and do not allow others to take advantage of or waste their time. They create barriers around their time by adding structure and systems into their businesses, which are respected by clients and peers. They clearly understand that time is their most valuable asset.

Unsuccessful people waste time doing unproductive things that don't allow for effective growth and give away their time too freely to others. Therefore, they create fewer income-generating opportunities.

5. They Own It!

Successful people build a solid business and brand foundation that sets them apart from the competition. They are known as experts and authorities within their respective industries. They own their business and their brand, which allows them to easily maximize their avenues to success.

Unsuccessful competitors do things like everyone else, lack a success plan to build on, or do just enough to survive.

6. They Think Differently Than the Average Person

Successful people think differently. They look one step into the future to see opportunity everywhere. They think outside the box and come up with creative and innovative ways of doing business.

Unsuccessful people follow the crowd or wait to copy other people's ideas, so they usually remain one step behind the competition.

7. They Love What They Do

Successful people don't think of work as work. They take pleasure in their business and love what they do for a living. This gives them a sense of achievement and happiness that fulfills their definition of success.

Unsuccessful people see work as survival and work to earn a living. Most don't enjoy what they do for a living and consider it a J-O-B.

The Number-One Problem That Doesn't Guarantee Success

Anyone can create ambition, drive, and determination to succeed. All these traits will move a person toward success, but they don't guarantee it.

Many people say they want success but actually don't because it means remaining fully committed, focusing too much, and being coachable and open to success!

Many say they want more success and more money, but they're too lazy to get off their asses and take action!

Others would rather complain about why it's too hard, so why even bother trying? The list of excuses is never-ending. Yet the bottom line is that they may talk a good game, but they don't really want success badly enough to go after it!

An important thing to know about success is that if you don't go after it, it's not coming to find you! Success comes with a certain amount of responsibility that not everyone is willing or able to accept. This stops many people from going for it.

You just can't hesitate, quit, or make excuses—period. Once you accept this, you can make a strong commitment to creating success in your life, and you will realize how much power you hold.

When you remain open to success, amazing opportunities will show up for you every day.

The Word "Success" Holds Power

You have the fundamental right to become more successful and earn all the money and prosperity you desire. But you must own it in your mind first.

Repeat the power word "success" frequently. Hold all the faith and conviction in the world when saying it. Your subconscious mind will catch up and start believing it, too. And when it does, it will lead you to success.

Tell yourself: I am successful—I am successful—I am successful!

The words you speak hold power and truth. When you use positive words about yourself and your ability to succeed, they will have an external effect. Likewise, if you continually make negative declarations about yourself or your business that evoke hopelessness, incite fear, or create anxiety, then those words will shape your reality. So pay close attention to what you say.

Not only do your words affect your opportunities for success, but they impact how others perceive and relate to you as well. If you often feel overlooked or undervalued, consider how your language may be contributing. Instead of framing what you say into limiting "cannots," consider limitless possibilities. For example, as someone who speaks at conferences around the world, I've had dozens of people say to me, "I could never do you what you do," or, "Public speaking scares me to death." Of course, not everyone feels compelled to be a public speaker, yet using limiting language like "never" and "scared to death" will only limit your success potential.

Decide to Choose from This Day Forward

You are 100 percent in control of the words in your head and the words coming out of your mouth. Choosing to use powerful words will continue to amplify your success-generating opportunities. When you realize just how capable you are—when you are more aware of the words you use every day—you can decide which words hold power and which words will greatly impact your success.

You can choose to:

- *Turn negative thoughts into positive ones.* Positive thoughts can literally change your brain. In simple terms, hearing and using positive thoughts and language can make you feel great—physically, mentally, and emotionally. On the flip side, negative thoughts and language can block the brain's natural de-stress mechanisms, which can cause you to worry and get stuck.

- *Use words that move you forward instead of limiting you.* You can find your limits by exposing yourself to different situations and pushing through the uncomfortable ones. Once you have confidence in yourself, you'll be amazed at what you can accomplish. The more confident words you use, the more you will continue to move forward.

- *Focus on opportunities instead of making excuses.* Opportunity occurs when you embrace possibilities. By refusing to allow difficulties to get in the way of your success, you create your own opportunities. Yet too many people wait for an opportunity to come to them or make excuses that the timing is not right. Excuses are simply our fears telling us that we are not capable of success: that we aren't good enough, smart enough, or strong enough to reach our goals. When you push past the difficulties and rise above your excuses, you will be able to see the opportunities available to you.

- *Remain coachable to new ideas vs. stuck on limiting beliefs.* You probably started your own business so you could be the captain of your ship and do things your own way. So why is it so important to remain coachable? The answer is simple: You don't have all the answers—no one does—and getting better at what you do is necessary to succeed. However, when business owners say they want to get better—attend seminars, read all the latest business books, and even hire a coach or consultant—too often what I see is lots of time and money being put in but the same business owner with limited beliefs comes out. They're often stuck in counterproductive behaviors that keep their businesses in a perpetual state of challenge. Cash-flow issues, unnecessary drama, excuses and blaming, playing the victim, and—worst of all—denial of the problems they've created. The best business owners remain coachable to new ideas at all times. That's what keeps them learning, growing, and succeeding.

- *Reinforce positive change vs. remaining the same.* First, you must identify and understand what you want to change. Start by identifying what is important to you and define your core values. What is it about your goal that adds to you as a person, that makes you feel better, more expansive, and more successful? When your goal aligns with your core values, your thoughts will trigger positive ambition and drive.

Choose Success or Failure

Hopefully you are beginning to understand how important it is to think and act differently to achieve more. You may be thinking, "If the power is already inside me to control my destiny and achieve success, why the heck don't I have all the success and money I want yet?"

There are concrete reasons you haven't already achieved the level of success you truly desire. Therefore, it's important to be aware of some misguided beliefs and bad habits around success that can lead to pitfalls and failures, which may have been perceived as beyond your control until now.

First, recognize that some timeless success principles can backfire. Most of the time, these principles backfire because of the invisible walls used to block them out—walls built from your own limiting beliefs. To make a shift, first become aware of the existing belief and try observing patterns more positively.

Success principles can also backfire if you have a black-and-white approach to beliefs about success. For example, many people believe you can only succeed or fail—there is no middle ground. The reality is that success is a bit fuzzy at times. To become more successful at anything, you must also learn from mistakes as you fail.

 Failure is simply part of the process of learning to succeed in business and in life.

Unsuccessful people see failure, freak out, and give up too soon, before they have a chance to succeed. This behavior can sabotage opportunities that are right in front of you. When this happens, you tend to get in your own way, make excuses, and stop taking action. Worst of all, you often buy into limiting beliefs that caused the failure in the first place.

For example, I have witnessed hundreds of people give up on success in a matter of minutes. After I speak at events, I often have a table set up at the back of the room to talk with audience members once I come off stage. Some attendees will wait in line for up to two hours to speak to me for two minutes. And most of the time, we talk about their failures.

At these events, I'm extremely intuitive about reading people. Often I can tell if someone will choose success or failure in just a couple of minutes, just through their body language and the words they use to describe their goals and business. Most seem to truly want success and value my advice, but far too many still choose failure. These people wait hours to talk with me, only to share excuses, problems, or—even worse—just to tell me about being "broke."

Yikes—I cringe when I hear that word. It's one of the most negative and limiting words anyone can use when it comes to sabotaging their personal success.

It amazes me what people will reveal when they want you to buy into their stories of misery and failure. Often they just want to remain stuck in their story. Sorry, but that doesn't work for me. I have no tolerance for self-limiting pity parties. What I have learned is that people who choose failure over success are not ready to hear positive reinforcement, innovative ideas, or useful advice.

I care about helping others succeed, but I can only help those who are ready to listen, learn, and take action. If this sounds good, keep reading. I'm here to help!

Success Is Easy Reality Check

What you may have learned about success when you were growing up was probably wrong if it was taught by someone who never actually achieved any real success of their own. Often you have to fail your way into learning to be successful.

Limiting beliefs around success can get in your way for far too long. It's time to take 100 percent responsibility for your success and make a strong commitment to making things happen in a big way.

You can choose winning over losing. Choose to succeed even when you fail by learning from the experience. Choose to learn from your mistakes and move on. Choose to win by grabbing hold of success from this day forward and never letting go. We should always be true to the best within ourselves!

Success is easy,
unless you choose to
make it hard!

Shameless, No-Nonsense Action Steps and Affirmation

Success Is Easy Affirmation (say it, believe it, and own it): "Success comes easy to me because I have a new reality around success to believe in from this day forward."

Now take these five steps to start wrapping your mind around the idea of success:

1. *Study the strengths and habits of other highly successful people and learn how to create a success-driven, ambitious mindset.* Successful people are simply those who have successful habits. Whether we like it or not, a big part of what we do in life is governed by habits. They can lead us to think and feel in certain patterns; they can also make us feel ambitious and motivated to succeed. Successful people know nothing can take the place of persistence and determination, so they make a habit of never quitting until they get results. The world's greatest achievers are those who have the willpower to stay focused on their goals and consistent in their efforts.

2. *Learn how to create a new reality that success is easy for you to achieve.* A dream without action is a world of make-believe. Success can be easy unless you choose to make it hard. Don't believe the myth that success comes from hard work alone. After all, without motivation, you can't get anything done. And even if you have all the motivation in the world, you need ambition to achieve a worthy goal.

3. *Repeat the word "success" frequently with complete faith and conviction; believe it to be true.* What you learned about success growing up was probably not true if it was taught by someone who never actually achieved it. Limiting beliefs and words around success can get in our way for far too long. It's time to take 100 percent responsibility for your success and make a strong commitment to making things happen in a big way!

4. *Pay close attention to the words you speak every day and choose empowering words from this day forward.* Not only do your words affect your success opportunities, but they impact how others perceive and relate to you as well. Instead of framing your words into limiting "cannots," turn them into non-limiting words to empower more success.

5. *Get off your ASS and really go for it!* You can choose winning over losing. You can choose to succeed even when you fail. You can choose to learn from your mistakes and move on. You can choose to win by grabbing hold of success from this day forward and never letting go. You should always be true to the best within yourself. Don't ever give up on the shameless pursuit of success. Period!

SUCCESS IS EASY . . .
with Definition

Here's a little secret: You can have whatever you want in life as long as you are willing to plan, focus, and execute. It's that easy!

When you were young, you were curious. You explored, reached out, and believed in things without explanation or proof. You felt like you could do anything, go anywhere, be whoever you wanted to be when you grew up.

As you got older, you might have been taught that you were not supposed to speak up or stand out. You

Repeat this mantra to yourself
as an affirmation:
"I am born to be a winner! I am born
fearless! I am born to be whatever
I want to be! Success is
waiting for me!"

might have been told to "stop dreaming," "be reasonable," and "not set your expectations too high."

What?

Does any of this nonsense sound familiar? These are false limitations fed into your belief system by others who were fed these same ideas, too. It's time to stop this madness. As an adult with your own life, choices, and beliefs, these limiting, negative, and false beliefs do not serve you and will sabotage your future opportunities for success.

Limiting beliefs can cause smart people to say really dumb things. Ever heard someone say, "I really don't care about being successful, I just need enough money to get by," "I'm broke," or "I'm just trying to keep my head above water"?

Again, that's nonsense! Why would someone limit themselves to such low standards? Doing so bankrupts their dreams of success. Unfortunately, many children grew up with parents and teachers who most likely didn't realize these ideas could limit their chances for success. And if you were unable to create your own strong belief system about success, you may have continued to believe this nonsense!

In this chapter, you will learn how to define success on your own terms. You will also discover that if you believe success is hard, you may just be going after it the wrong way. You will begin to realize that when you define your own success, you will know how it feels when you succeed. There is no limit to the amount of success that's available to you.

Forget About Fear and Get Back into the Winner's Circle

If fear or doubt stops you from being the winner you were born to be, it's up to you to turn it around and get back into the winner's circle where you belong. Over time, whether you realize it or not, fear and doubt can steal success. You must fight to get back into the winner's circle and stay there.

Fear does not protect you. Instead, it creates a person who can't act or take risks due to uncertainty or doubt. Fear holds you back from being a high performer. It makes you feel inadequate and may even make you think you are not good enough to succeed. Fears are false beliefs—but they appear real to you.

Do not tolerate for one minute the idea that an absence of inborn talent or ability will stop you from achieving great things. Never let fear win over the reality that you are born a winner!

Prepare to Win

Before you define what success looks like for you, remember that you are hard-wired to succeed. Success is a birthright. You are put on this earth to be successful. Never apologize for that. A person who is 100 percent committed to success cannot fail.

I believe everyone arrives here on earth with a mission, and once you discover who you are and what you truly want out of life, nothing can stop you. Hold on to the belief that you can achieve whatever you put your mind to. There is no way anyone can stop you unless you allow it to happen.

Most people don't realize that they already have the ability to accomplish almost anything they set their mind to. This ability lies within you and is just waiting to be released.

No matter how many detours you've taken or unexpected delays you've encountered, that path has inevitably been leading you to one place—success.

Most people search high and low for the success that is already inside them. You are different because you are open to an enlightened understanding of what success actually is. It's the most essential thing you have been searching for.

Don't wait for something to inspire you to feel successful. If you wait, you may miss the momentum and the opportunities that are just around the corner. Don't wait to see how you perform or what you accomplish so you can look successful in the eyes of others. Success has already chosen you. You just have to choose it in return.

Success is a choice that you make from moment to moment. Each day and each minute, you can choose success over failure. You just need to recognize it and then give yourself permission to feel successful.

Success never creates discomfort. It's your inner battle with success that makes you feel uncomfortable. When you try to suppress success in your subconscious, you actually push success opportunities away from you. I see this all the time—people sabotaging their success opportunities because they feel uncomfortable going for it. Some people say they want to expand and achieve more success, but they reach a certain level and stop themselves. There are many reasons for this, but one of the main ones is that they have subconsciously chosen to play small. Why? Because some part of them knows they can't handle the responsibility and experiences that success requires of them. Although they say they want more success, they don't actually want the added exposure, pressure, and accomplishment. They would rather remain small and where they consider safe than push themselves to achieve more. Often they say they want success but are afraid it will be too uncomfortable for them, so when they suddenly begin to expand they choose to slow down or even run from it altogether.

For example, I personally coached a smart young woman who wanted success and independence in her career. She had big dreams and plans to achieve a high level of success. At the beginning of our work together, her big dreams drove her to find answers and to invest heavily in her own success. But within a few months, after gaining traction and momentum in her business development, she began to slow down the process and halt her progress. She began to focus on small details and move away from big leaps that would produce better results. She began to sabotage opportunities because the reality of succeeding at a higher level caused her to panic and retreat.

The problem was that once she started to achieve more, she felt that lasting success would create added pressure and responsibility that she would have to maintain. She also began to worry about what others might think of her if she tried to play a bigger game. She ultimately decided to quit trying and went back to playing at a smaller level she had learned to feel comfortable with.

Unfortunately we can all sabotage success, even when we think success is what we want most in life. To move away from self-sabotage, you must learn to expand your capacity for success, wisdom, and power. If you don't, you will continue to retreat and sabotage your progress. Once you learn how to expand your capacity to achieve more, succeed more, and win more often, success becomes easier.

Don't worry about gathering all the information and details before deciding to become more successful. You don't need all the answers, and you don't need to know the "how" right now. Once you are ready, the "how" will begin to appear for you.

For now, it's time to move forward with your beliefs around success. Stop worrying about how you will look and what others may think of you. It's time to begin acting as if you have already achieved the success you desire—even if you have to fake it before you make it!

Define What Success Means

The number-one reason most people don't succeed is that they don't take the time to define what they want. One of the most important things for you is to know exactly what you want. What does success look like or feel like to you? If you don't know, you attract confusion.

Success is not what others tell you it is. It's what you say it is for yourself!

If you believe success is what everyone else says it is, you'll always miss the target. And when you do achieve someone else's version of success, it won't mean as much to you.

Succeeding requires giving up other people's beliefs around success. Forget about what other people think about success and stop comparing yourself to them. Some people think success is defined as having tons of money, fame, and fortune. The reality is that success is defined in many ways, but it must come from within to motivate true success on your terms.

By understanding and valuing who you are and why you desire success, it's easier to tap into your true value by becoming more aware of your strengths, skills, and existing knowledge. Some valuable qualities may have come to you as naturally born talent; these are called gifts. Skills are learned and developed over time with effort and experience.

To help figure out your value, think of a time when you were completely "dialed-in," a time when you felt as if you were completely in your element or in "the zone." How did it feel in that moment? What strengths, skills, and knowledge came easily to you?

Learn to listen to your inner promptings for the kind of success you desire. This allows you to start out feeling challenged in the best possible way. Chances are that when you take stock of your strengths and consider all possibilities for success, you will discover there is more than one path to getting there. You may also discover there is something else you want more, or another area that is a stronger market or a higher chance of success. This will allow you to stop wasting time on opportunities that aren't right for you. You want to be able to decide what you most want for yourself!

Success on Your Own Terms

Defining your own success means knowing why you want it. For example, when you say, "I want success!" what do you really want?

Taking ownership of your success means taking full responsibility for your direction. If you are going to spend the rest of your life doing something, it should be something you really want to do.

Successful, high-performing people look at what they want and move forward until they achieve it. The main goal is to live a life you're proud of and to achieve a level of success that's worth fighting for.

It doesn't matter where you start from. It only matters that you want it badly enough to fight for it when challenged. Only you know what you're willing to fight for.

> **!** Your success is NOT defined by others—it's only defined by yourself. Success is defined by knowing what you want most in life, and most of all, believing that you can achieve it.

Success Is Not One Size Fits All

You may believe success is defined by money, fame, happiness, material items, etc. But success does not come with a one-size-fits-all label. Success must be defined by your own labels.

The meaning of success is different for each person. You may not fit into other people's definition of success, but you can give yourself permission to be OK with that. Success is an individual concept. I cannot define success for anyone else. I can only define it for myself. But here's the exciting part: You get to define and design your own success, which will become the blueprint for you to follow throughout your life. Developing your own success blueprint also means that you get to create success on your own terms.

While writing this book, I asked hundreds of people to define what the word "success" meant to them in their own terms. Almost every person gave me a different definition. For example, when I asked Vanessa Campos of Entrepreneur Press, she said, "Defining success is like the adult version of 'What do you want to be when you grow up?'" I found her statement very insightful.

What Do You Want to Be When You Grow Up?

Remember being asked as a child, "What do you want to be when you grow up?" As children you are allowed to dream and define your own success story any way you want. So why do we stop asking ourselves that question?

It's extremely challenging to manage your actions toward success if you haven't identified and defined it first. You can actually be highly successful and still feel like a failure if you do not clearly define what success means to you.

For example, if you only measure success in dollars, you may always be looking for that bigger pot of gold at the end of a new rainbow. Working harder, working faster, and doing more are not necessarily the keys to achieving personal satisfaction and success. You may even measure success by comparing yourself to others. Even with a hefty bank account and a financially free lifestyle, you may still feel like a failure when everyone around you sees you as successful. This definition of success is dangerous because you may set yourself up for false failure based on unfair comparisons and personal judgments. Instead, create your own definition of what success means to you.

Three Steps to Define Success

Although definitions of success are subjective, the process of defining it is quite objective.

First, begin by clearly defining what you want so you can see the final outcome. Here are three steps to directing yourself toward success.

Step 1: Discover Why Success Is Important to You

To discover why success is important to you, ask yourself these important questions. Take out a piece of paper and answer the following questions in as much detail as possible:

- Is your success defined with professional achievements, personal happiness, and/or financial freedom?

- How will achieving more success make you feel? (For example: more confident, more empowered, fearless, etc.)
- After achieving more success, how will your life be different than it is right now? Would you live in a different city, have a completely different career, take more vacations, etc.?
- How will you apply the principles defined and outlined for you in this book? As you read through this book, be sure to highlight the areas you most need to focus on and work toward to achieve a higher level of success.

Step 2: Uncover Your Drive to Move Past Obstacles

Achieving more success requires you to become more driven and persistent when challenges and obstacles get in the way. The journey is challenging as you learn, grow, and experience more. As obstacles arise, you must take full responsibility to stay on course. Ask yourself:

- What obstacles prevent you from achieving success?
- How will removing these obstacles help you move forward to achieving a higher level of success?
- How can you then hold yourself accountable for staying on course to achieving the desired level of success?
- What action steps have you avoided in the past that could have helped you achieve more?

Once you define the action steps that are required to achieve more and understand what's holding you back, you can finally begin to make big strides as you remain in action. Action is required to move you beyond obstacles. When the going gets tough, you need to remain in action to knock down obstacles, climb over barriers, or move beyond anything that gets in your way.

Step 3: Start by Taking the First Step

Too many people want to start a business but postpone the decision while looking for the perfect business idea that will make millions. Often the only reason many don't take action on their planned goals and dreams is lack of confidence in their abilities. The only solution to this problem is to start. Self-confidence won't build itself. *Success Is Easy* but only if you start.

It doesn't matter if you know how to succeed at something or how to achieve your goals. You don't need to figure it all out before you start. Not knowing how to do something has never stopped me from starting a new business venture or from reaching for success before I knew how. I simply started. I took the first step and kept on going.

I'm a strong believer in the idea that anyone can become successful at just about anything—when they set their mind to it and get started. Even if you take the wrong step, readjust, step in a new direction, and start again. Consider the following questions:

- What could you start doing tomorrow if you knew you couldn't fail?
- If the lack of knowledge were not holding you back, what would you step into tomorrow?
- If there were no fear or doubt holding you back, what bold action steps could you take to achieve more success?
- If you were told you could not stop until you achieved your goal, what big goal would you reach for?

Here's an example. When I was ready to begin hiking out of the Grand Canyon after a fun week of rafting down the Colorado River, our tour guide said, "Remember to keep a positive mindset on your journey because this is probably one of the most physically challenging things you'll ever do. It's more about mindset than anything else. Just keep a positive mindset and keep putting one foot in front of the other." I thought that it would be easy enough because I believed that I had a positive mindset until I realized how extremely hard it was going to be. The guide also said, "You can't give up when it comes to achieving your goal because if you quit, the park rangers will come down and rescue you, but they will charge you thousands of dollars and then put you back on the trail to finish your climb. Therefore, don't plan on quitting!"

What if you had a guide like this with you every day, one who told you you couldn't quit no matter what? Would you achieve more? Of course you would! So as your guide today, I ask you . . . what goal would you achieve if you knew you couldn't quit?

Get Out of Your Own Way

If your goal is as vague as "success" or "money," you will have a challenging time trying to harness it. This will make it seem as if success is hard, but it shouldn't be. If it feels hard, you are doing it wrong.

The no-nonsense bottom line is that if what you are doing is not working, you must be open to a new way of doing things. This is simply good business sense.

If success feels too challenging, walk away from what is not working, shift your actions, and rethink the situation altogether. Set aside any personal emotions that may cloud your judgment on why things may not be working right now.

Remove anything else that may influence false perceptions around your level of success. In other words, start by getting out of your own way.

Step outside your wants and get to the results you are looking for. This is the best way for you to get at the true essence of your personal definition of success: focus on the final outcome you are trying to achieve.

Shameless, No-Nonsense Action Steps and Affirmation

Success Is Easy Affirmation (say it, believe it, and own it): "Success comes easy to me because I now define success on my own terms."

1. *If fear or doubt stops you from being the winner you were born to be, it's up to you to turn it around and get back into the winner's circle where you belong.* Once you do, stay there by eliminating any limited beliefs that success may be too hard

for you to achieve. Get back into the winner's circle prepared to win now!

2. *Realize that you already have the ability to accomplish almost anything you set your mind to.* You were born a winner! You were born fearless! You were born to be whatever you want to be! Success is waiting for you!

3. *Listen to inner promptings for hints of the kind of success you desire.* Take stock of your strengths and consider all possibilities for success. Define your own success by truly understanding and valuing who you are and why you want to succeed. It's easier to tap into our true value when we become more aware of our strengths, skills, and existing knowledge. Success is defined in many ways, but you must look within to create or motivate true success on your own terms. Becoming successful requires giving up other people's beliefs around success.

4. *Take complete ownership of your success.* When you say, "I want success," what are you really asking for? Why is success important to you? Do you define it with professional achievements, personal happiness, and/or financial wealth? Will achieving more success make you "feel" different? Will you be more confident, more empowered, more fearless, etc.?

5. *If what you are doing now is not working, you must be open to new ways of doing things.* If success appears hard or challenging to you, it's time to shift your actions and rethink your position altogether. Start by setting aside emotions that may cloud your judgment on why things may not be working right now. Remove anything else that may influence false perceptions around your ability to achieve success. In other words, start by getting out of your own way so you can make some real and lasting progress.

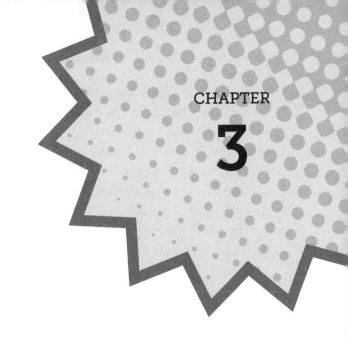

SUCCESS IS EASY . . .
with the Right Mindset

M any people say they want success, but they don't act like it. Why? Because they don't want to take the necessary actions to create success. For example, many want the results of success, but not the responsibility that goes along with achieving it.

The truth is that success is easier than failure! With all the knowledge, education, and training available today, it's actually harder to fail than to succeed.

So why settle for failure? Because success scares some people. They settle because they have a subconscious fear of success. When negative or false beliefs are fed into someone's subconscious mind, they turn it into self-sabotage. This often happens when someone is creating change or moving forward in life. Fear to some people feels real because that belief is deeply instilled in them. Yet to create and sustain success, it is critical to release the belief in the fear of success altogether. If you don't overcome your false belief, it will begin to control you.

In this chapter, you will learn how to create the right mindset to allow more success to flow to you. You will find out how to uncover limiting and false beliefs around success that may be holding you back. And you will discover how to get out of the "lame excuse zone" that keeps most people stuck, unhappy, and unsuccessful. Learn to keep your attitude in check and keep moving forward despite all odds.

Say No to F.E.A.R.

F.E.A.R. (False Evidence Appearing Real) comes from the false beliefs and myths around the meaning of success. Yet all fear can vanish once you own your beliefs and discover the real truth about success.

Once you define your own success with new beliefs, there is nothing to fear. So let's look at a few false beliefs or myths that contribute to failure.

False Belief #1: Success is all about power, wealth, and fame.

People who measure success only in terms of power, wealth, and fame are looking in the wrong place. When someone believes you must measure up to those high standards, you may not even want to try.

Here's the reality: Success is about feeling confident, empowered, and committed to your core values. Your values are part of your overall success equation. Successful people stay connected to their self by tapping into what they value most about themselves and their business.

False Belief #2: Success is hard work and takes forever to achieve.

People who believe that it takes too long or that it's too hard to achieve success will lose motivation and commitment to take action. But that's not you!

If success seems too far out in the future or even unattainable, people will start to make up excuses for why it won't work. But you've already seen that excuses don't work.

Here's the reality: Working hard for a long period of time does not guarantee success. In fact, success can happen quickly and easily. If you have the right skills or talent, you can succeed with minimum effort. You can experience success easily every day through small achievements, accomplishments, and personal growth.

False Belief #3: Successful people are selfish and self-centered.

Those who believe successful people are selfish or self-centered usually feel uncomfortable standing out in a crowd and may also fear self-promotion. A person who believes this often feels that putting yourself out there will cause others to judge you as rude, pushy, or intrusive.

Here's the reality: You won't find truly successful people focusing internally. They know how to self-promote effectively in the service of others. The only way to truly be successful is to get comfortable standing out and promoting your value, services, and ideas.

False Belief #4: You need a formal education to succeed.

Some people believe getting a college diploma or another degree will make you successful. Some actually work hard at becoming professional students, while piling up debt. Others use the excuse that it's critically important to learn more before going out into the world and taking action. In the meantime, they will hold back from going after success until they feel "ready."

Here's the reality: You don't need a formal education to prepare you for success. It can sometimes be the slower route. The most expensive university will only give you the tools to help you learn and grow. It's still up to you to come up with a plan and execute it. Education comes in many forms and can be gained in a variety of ways. The key is to absorb knowledge and gain life experiences that will teach you how to apply your wisdom.

False Belief #5: Negative thinking patterns cannot be changed.

When you engage in habitual negative thinking, positive thoughts will not come naturally or easily until you choose to change your thoughts.

Here's the reality: All thinking patterns can be changed, even negative ones. Once negative thinking turns to more positive thoughts, it creates a greater sense of success. The more someone trains the brain to think in positive ways, the more it's expected, acted on, and achieved.

Quit Stopping the Flow of Success

Your F.E.A.R. can hold you back and stop your natural flow of success thanks to these kinds of false beliefs. Let me ask you this: "Do you want me to tell you what you want to hear or what you need to hear?" If a person is ready to listen, I'll be upfront and honest. We all stop success from flowing to us at some level. The only thing standing between you and more success is yourself! Therefore, ask yourself these questions, journal the answers, and keep the responses at top of mind to help address what's holding you back:

- Has fear held you back from the success you deserve in any way?
- Have you crushed your own dreams of success in the past?
- Have you destroyed advantages for success opportunities?

If failure crushes your spirit, it makes you play a smaller game in business and in life.

Unfortunately, many people all over the world feel stuck and ultimately give up. Yet to achieve success, you need to succeed on your own. You are responsible for everything that happens. That may be a hard pill to swallow, but unless you accept it, you cannot change things for the better.

Your biggest enemy is the person you see when you look in the mirror. It's not your lack of education, financial situation, or the bad decisions you've made in the past that are holding you back. It's you!

Let's identify some ways you can change your mindset to reflow success in your direction.

Control Your Thoughts Around Success

Controlling your thoughts is the hardest part of struggling toward success. It's a big challenge. You must become mentally tough!

If you allow fear to drive your thoughts, you'll never do the challenging things that lead to success. You must learn how to use fear to push you toward more creativity, more passion, and more purpose.

Learn to change self-sabotaging thoughts and habits and eliminate the excuses that keep you stuck or unproductive. If you dwell on negative thoughts for too long, they will control you. In fact, your thoughts are so powerful, they can determine the level of success you achieve more than the actual actions you take.

Negative thoughts can be self-defeating regardless of how hard you try. Once someone has accepted a false belief as fact, all the well-intentioned efforts and willpower in the world are no match for it.

Keep the Attitudes in Check

Attitudes are extremely important in determining the difference between success and failure. Your attitudes either support you or keep you from positive change, depending on how you use them. Experiences lead you to believe certain things about yourself, whether or not they're true. If you accept them as true, then these false beliefs are true for you. There is then nothing you can do except work to change your thinking.

Move Outside the Limitation Zone

Plant a seed and it will grow. Unfortunately, negative attitudes and beliefs can grow to become limitations. The sad thing is that even though you know your life isn't working in certain areas, you may still be afraid to change. You can become locked into an "uncomfortable" comfort zone. I refer to this as a "limitation zone." The only way to get out of this zone is to free yourself of the limitations holding you there.

To move outside the limitation zone, you must stop lying to yourself about what's not working, stop blaming others for your problems, and stop avoiding unpleasant decisions that keep you from acting. To step outside to a better life, you must face the truth that you have accepted unworkable beliefs that are the direct cause for the challenges in your life.

Moving outside your limitation zone is a matter of changing your mind toward more positive and productive thinking, and moving toward knowing the absolute truth about who you really are.

Be on High Alert for the Lame Excuse Zone

Negative self-talk kills opportunities for success. You must remain on high alert for damaging self-talk that creates extreme limitations, throwing you into the "lame excuse zone." This zone is where no one takes responsibility for success. Ever heard these lame excuses?

- "If it wasn't for bad luck, I wouldn't have any luck at all."
- "I feel like a total failure."
- "I'll try to figure it out, but I'm so bad at . . ."
- "I don't need to make much money."
- "I'm broke!"

Limiting words such as these can leave anyone feeling hopeless. Stop it! They are simply lame excuses for playing small.

Using words like these will cause you to unconsciously sabotage your success. When you find yourself stuck in negative and limiting storytelling, you hold yourself back from success and alienate yourself from others. Let it go! Drop it! No one wants to hear your lame poor-me stories anyway. This may sound harsh, but I want to show you the tremendous power words have when it comes to choosing success over failure.

Limiting words are dream-killers and stress-makers. They imply that you have no choice, no options, no freedom, and no control. They let you pretend that you are a victim. We all use limiting words out of habit. Listen for them very carefully and purge them from your vocabulary.

Don't Tolerate Excuses!

Just as limiting words will stifle your success, so too will excuses. It's time to remove self-sabotaging excuses that keep you stuck.

Stop making excuses for who and where you are in life. Often it's just a rationalization for not taking action or being downright lazy. Lazy is for losers. Losers don't want to make the effort required to succeed.

You have attracted everything that has come into your life: good or bad, happy or sad, success or failure. If you want to change your life and attract something different, it's time to to stop excuses from forming in the first place. Successful people consider every situation an opportunity, even when it appears limiting or hopeless to a negative person. Learn to do the same to attract more success into your life.

Think of it this way. In the amount of time it takes for the mind to come up with a lame excuse, it could have created another way to achieve the desired result, rendering excuse-making completely unnecessary. Learn to live "excuse-free" and take full responsibility for every aspect of your life. Start creating a future you're excited about and proud of.

It starts with believing you can be amazing regardless of who or where you are in life right now.

Training and managing your own mind is the most important skill you can have for success and happiness. Separate yourself from negativity and learn to become more positive. A negative person is mentally weak. It takes no mental courage to have negative thoughts. What does take mental effort—and lots of it—is to find the best in every situation and stop making excuses for what goes wrong.

One way you can start to do that is by choosing your words carefully.

Manifest Success with Words

The words you speak hold immense power to fuel your confidence and ambition—or shut you down. They can help you make a great first impression or guarantee you are ignored.

To gain more confidence and success opportunities, begin with what you're projecting to yourself and others every time you open your mouth.

Words carry an energy that subtly—or not so subtly—changes their meaning from moment to moment and day to day. No dictionary will ever tell you this. Only your experience and common sense will allow you to discover it for yourself.

Avoid Negative Thoughts and Emotions Around Money

Someone with a scarcity mindset around money is challenged when it comes to achieving success. People without money often feel victimized, but they are creating and living a self-fulfilling prophecy by constantly complaining about and condemning the things they claim to desire: success and money. Speaking critically of what you want is not creating positive success.

On the other hand, someone with a prosperity mindset will attract money and income-generating opportunities like a magnet. This is why the rich get richer and the poor get poorer. People with winning self-beliefs do things that allow them to keep winning. And when they lose, they don't accept it as fate. They pick themselves up and keep going.

One of the fastest ways to repel money is to criticize anything or anyone who has more than you do. Another way is to believe you don't deserve it. When this happens, you will find a way to rid yourself of money as quickly as possible, even when you say it's what you desire most. Unfortunately, most people have to learn this the hard way by overspending, making poor financial decisions, or making bad investments.

LEARNING LESSONS ABOUT SUCCESS AND MONEY FROM YOUR PARENTS

For many people, their parents are where they first learn about success—and money in particular. Limiting beliefs around success and money held my father back from having what he said he wanted most in life—success! Although he was obsessed with finding success, he subconsciously sabotaged his opportunities. He had great success in our family car rental and mini-storage business in the 1970s, but after selling these two businesses, he struggled to find success again. His obsession continued his entire life.

For decades, he made extremely impulsive financial decisions. Money found him many times, but he always allowed it to slip away instead of investing it wisely for the future. He would invest in any new business venture that came his way with little thought or research. Dozens of failed business startups later, he was still preoccupied with finding success.

My father's philosophy about money was to save his own (although he never actually did) and finance as much as possible. He called it the "American way." He never planned for the future. With every new business he started, he put little time or focus into building it. When he ran into an obstacle, he would drop it and move on to something else. I believe he became so obsessed with success that he started to ignore reality.

To this day, I ask myself, *Why would someone who wants success so badly continue to sabotage it? Why would someone settle for less, while looking for more in another direction? Why would someone ignore reality time and time again?*

LEARNING LESSONS, continued

Parents are the first people to teach us about life, money, and success. As adults, we can choose to either follow the same path or find our own way. But you need to make very certain that you don't inadvertently learn lessons that don't serve you well. I didn't discover my own self-sabotaging money lesson until later in life.

Much of what I learned came from working in a family business I invested in when I was 19 years old. My father and mother taught me a lot about business at a young age, and I'm very grateful. Some of their lessons were good and some were bad, but even the bad ones taught me a lot about what *not* to do in business. I learned to pay very close attention to what didn't work as much as what did work.

My mom's biggest lesson for me was to have a strong work ethic. Although she always worked hard, she still didn't have great success on her own. This taught me at an early age that although hard work is important, you need much more than that to be successful.

My dad's biggest lesson for me was to remain focused. When he focused on one business at a time and stuck with it, it succeeded. When he started a new business but put little focus or energy into it, it failed every time. This taught me to remain focused and to keep putting energy into a business until it succeeded. This lesson has paid off for me many times over.

But some lessons took me longer to learn. After building and selling my own retail stores for 15 years, I started looking for my next career opportunity. I sold my last retail store and then had the time and money to focus on my professional speaking career. After a few years, my new career began to take off, and I started to make big money. But I also started spending big, too. I bought an expensive house, a brand-new luxury sports car, and expensive clothing. I also did lots of expensive travel. Money was flowing quickly in and out of my bank account. And I was not saving money or making plans for my future.

Then, after a weekend at a money mindset workshop, I started asking myself questions that created a new awareness around my behavior: "Wait a minute, what are you doing? Why are you allowing money to slip away so quickly? Are you not comfortable having so much of it?"

I realized I had subconsciously started to self-sabotage my money flow. It was partly because I had followed the same pattern of behavior that my father had. And I also had not yet learned

Choose to Stay Stuck in the Past or Move Forward

If you ask the average person about their thinking patterns and beliefs around money, the response may be, "My thoughts and beliefs come from the way I was brought up." This is simply another lame excuse for overspending and staying stuck in the past.

What also keeps most people stuck is the false concepts, values, and beliefs they learned in childhood that prevent them from realizing how truly capable and valuable they are. To change this limited mindset, uncover new programming to discover your true worthiness, if you wish to achieve total self-confidence and fulfill your destiny of success.

Only you can decide whether to learn from your mistakes. Decide to make bad or good business and financial decisions.

Decide to have a scarcity mindset or a prosperity mindset. It's time to choose wisely.

Reject Doomsayers

If you want to remain committed to your passion and pave your own path toward success, you must ignore the "doomsayers," those people who only focus on the negative.

If you have ever shared a big goal with someone only to be told, "What makes you think you can do that?," "You'll never achieve that," or "You're crazy!," then you've met these doomsayers. It's easy to get discouraged when you're surrounded by people who shoot down your ideas, dreams, and goals. But you must learn to walk away from negative people whose opinions don't matter.

Ask yourself, "Why are they telling me this? Have they done it? Do they have experience in it?" If these people don't have real firsthand experience that can support you, avoid them altogether. Their opinion should mean nothing to you, because it's empty. Learn to replace doomsayers' and dream stealers' responses with positive feedback where you can.

You should always associate with people you feel worthy of being with. This includes friends as well as business clients. You draw to yourself what you feel worthy of receiving. When you associate with successful people, it expands your way of thinking, doing, and achieving.

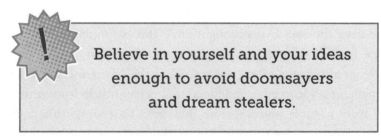

Believe in yourself and your ideas
enough to avoid doomsayers
and dream stealers.

Level Up Your Mindset for Success

When you change your mind, you change your world. I strongly believe that success and happiness have a great deal to do with your mindsets. Your mindset and belief system affect everything in your life, from what you think and feel to how you act and react to the world around you. To achieve your goals, your mindset needs to match your ambition. If it doesn't, it might be preventing you from getting where you want to be. Here are some ways to level up your mindset for more success.

Stop Comparing Yourself to Others

Comparing yourself to others sets you up for failure. This is why it's important to stay focused on what you're doing and not worry about comparing your progress to others. The only things that matter are where you are, what you're doing, and what conversations you are having with yourself.

The conversations you have with yourself are a direct reflection of your mindset. If you are telling yourself, "I am not good enough to achieve success," your thoughts will create your reality, and your mindset will hold you back from having the life you want. To level up your mindset, change your negative self-talk to an empowerment talk, such as, "I can do this," or "I got this." It really does help you focus on your goals, and that's what drives your success!

Practice Gratitude and Appreciate What You Have

Practice gratitude for your knowledge, skills, and experiences. When you are grateful for every opportunity placed in front of you, more will appear in the future. True happiness is about loving and respecting ourselves. Success will come as a natural extension of that.

Make an effort to appreciate your achievements. Don't just pay attention to what you're doing. Honor each and every one of your accomplishments. And if your friends don't appreciate your results right along with you, it may be time to find some new friends.

Decide now to be open, responsive, and receptive to new ideas and beliefs. Imagine success. Realize that your actions, feelings, and behaviors are the result of your beliefs.

One of the goals of this book is to get you to think differently and to open your mind to the idea that success really is easy. It's waiting for you just around the next corner. Believe that anything is possible even if it appears to be nearly inconceivable. Everything you think about, talk about, and act on thus becomes intentionally aligned with your purpose, values, and level of success.

If you are committed to success, you must have a whatever-it-takes attitude and a positive belief system.

Remain Committed to Success

When you are committed to changing your inner awareness and mindset, your outer circumstances change, too. It boils down to this: Decide what you want and believe you're going to get it. You can choose to discard your old script and focus on a completely new story. The new script will attract to you the people and the conditions to fulfill your dreams, goals, and desires.

As you practice more positive inner thoughts and beliefs, you also intuitively attract more magic into your life. You see this happen every day in nature. Nature is truly magical. For example, have you ever watched a bird build a nest? No one taught it how to do that—it relies solely on instinct. What you call instinct in animals is known as intuition in humans.

The same guiding intuition channeled into your beliefs will show you how to say the right words and take the right actions.

Once you are open to this idea, you learn to trust it and make fewer mistakes because you are guided to wiser and more intuitive choices. And believe me, you will start to become happier as well—naturally!

Win in Your Mind First

When you develop a positive mindset around success, you instantly begin to break down negative and limiting belief systems. Barriers and obstacles that once limited your success begin to disappear.

If you can remove these negative beliefs and replace them with affirmations for long enough, unlimited opportunities and abundance have a chance to blossom and grow. The idea behind affirmations is that through repeating positive statements, you can improve your self-respect and confidence. When you make progress toward personal growth and away from negative beliefs, you become a magnet for success.

Changing your mindset takes time; it doesn't happen overnight. Yet converting self-limiting and self-sabotaging beliefs into positive action every day will help guide you toward new skills and a more positive way of thinking and functioning.

A mindset shift will take you from drifting along unfocused, hoping for the best, to feeling enthusiastic and energetic and having an achievable action plan. This, in turn, attracts more success.

Shameless, No-Nonsense Action Steps and Affirmation

Success Is Easy Affirmation (say it, believe it, and own it): "Success comes easy to me because I have the right mindset to move past limiting beliefs and negative words that don't serve me."

1. *Stop sabotaging the flow of easy success with a limited mindset.* The main thing holding you back from achieving more success is you. With all the knowledge, education, and training available today, it's actually harder to fail than to succeed. So why would you ever settle for failure? To create and sustain success, it is critical to stop sabotaging yourself.

2. *Keep your attitude in check by being on high alert for the lame excuse zone that is holding you back from success opportunities.* Become mentally tough! Success has no tolerance for

excuses! All thinking patterns can be changed, even negative ones. Negative thoughts can get shifted into more positive ones. Once that happens, it creates a greater sense of success. The more you train your brain to think in positive ways, the more it's expected, acted on, and achieved.

3. *Move outside the limitation zone.* Learn how to control limiting beliefs and negative thoughts around your ability to succeed. Learn to change self-sabotaging thoughts and habits, and you'll begin to wipe out the excuses that keep you stuck or unproductive. If you dwell on negative thoughts for too long, they will control you. Your thoughts are so powerful that they—not your actions—can determine your level of success.

4. *Avoid negative beliefs and emotions around money and learn new lessons that support "abundance consciousness."* When you create a prosperity mindset, you will begin to attract money and income-generating opportunities like a magnet. People with winning mindsets do things that help them win more often.

5. *Be grateful for every opportunity placed in front of you, which allows success to flow to you easily.* The no-nonsense reality is that you can have anything you want—if you give up the belief that you can't have it. Within you is the ability to do whatever you need to do to be happy and successful. Within you is the power to do things you never dreamed were possible. This power becomes available as soon as you change your negative, limiting beliefs into empowered beliefs and positive words.

SUCCESS IS EASY . . .
when Failures Turn into Lessons

One common definition of success is continuously improving ourselves. As you build self-control and personal strength, you will also gain the knowledge you need to try new things. And when you do, you will sometimes make mistakes and fail.

Failure is valuable. It teaches you to turn your movement in a new direction. Yet the fear of failure can hold people back from moving forward. Many new business owners who fail at their first attempt become too fearful to try again. When this happens, they miss opportunities to learn and grow from their mistakes. Sadly, the failure probably was not caused by their inability to generate a good idea or manage a business. It may have been because they simply didn't take the time to figure out the problem and then gave up when fear set in.

This chapter will open your mind to new possibilities. You will discover that when you feel like giving up, you can just push a little harder and learn the lessons failure has to teach you. When you move past failure and learn from your mistakes, you will begin to experience the magic of success.

Your magical new realizations and awakenings will happen not because of the words in this book, but because of your personal experiences as you integrate the lessons you've learned and shift the direction of your actions.

Embrace Failure and Dysfunction

Failure and dysfunction go hand in hand. Take startups, for example. All new startups can be dysfunctional, but if you are willing to learn from dysfunction it can teach you a lot about business. Dysfunction taught me what actions caused the most failures, and from this I learned how to overcome failures to survive in business. Dysfunction also taught me right from wrong. From this I learned how to pay close attention to my mistakes and accept change.

Learn to embrace what your mistakes have to teach you. Become resourceful enough to overcome the dysfunction of any new business venture, because if you are waiting for everything to line up just right before you act, then you are achieving nothing but a foolproof excuse for failure.

If you don't learn from your mistakes, you will keep repeating the same bad business habits in other ventures. To truly learn from your failures, take a twofold approach: Don't dwell on your failures, and take ownership of them.

Don't Dwell on Failure

Failure can weigh heavily on you at times and may even limit your innate ability to succeed. When this happens, you must not allow your emotions to overpower you and stop you from acting. When successful people fail, they refocus on what's possible and continue on, despite any mistakes that try to get in the way.

To succeed in business, do not dwell on failures! Don't allow them to define you in any way. Losers focus on the hardship of failure; winners focus on the rewards of success.

Imagine what you could do if you didn't limit yourself. Stop playing to not lose and start playing to win from the start, every time, all the time, no matter how much failure tries to limit you. It comes down to this: You want success more than you want to accept failure.

Successful people play the business game to win even when they fail. Unsuccessful people play the game not to lose! When you are playing to win, you will do whatever you have to do to move things forward. You aggressively go after what you need to succeed. You take action and remain in motion!

Playing to win doesn't mean you are reckless, but you're certainly not passive about going after what you want. When you play to win, you do things that are uncomfortable or that you're afraid of, you speak your mind, and you move over obstacles as if there were no other option. You are playing full out! Your goal is to do whatever it takes to succeed.

Are you playing to win, or are you playing not to lose?

Take Ownership of Your Failures

While you shouldn't dwell on failure, you should honor it. What matters is to admit and accept the failure. Lying to yourself and others about failure will only delay the lessons you need to learn. Taking ownership of failures can free you from your mistakes and allow you to continue on with new and improved actions.

When you are willing to move beyond failure, your life and successes will become easier. You must learn not to fear things that appear challenging by sharpening your willpower and bridging the gap between where you are and where you want to be. Refocus on a clearer and more direct path to achieving results, which is typically the easiest, smoothest, and most realistic path of least resistance.

Invest in Winning from the Start

Every time I want to learn a new business model, I invest in a successful person who is already doing what I most want to learn about. I learn how to do things better, faster, and easier from that person and implement those lessons. This cuts my learning curve down dramatically and moves me closer to success sooner. I believe that if you want to learn how to do something well, you must take advice and guidance from those who have already done it very well. Why try to figure it out on your own? Would you learn about success from someone who has had limited success themselves or study under someone who has had years of success, time and time again? And when you meet someone who can teach you, you should be open to investing in yourself and your future to learn faster. It's common sense to keep investing where you see the greatest return. When you have a chance to invest in knowledge from someone who has already walked the path you wish to follow, you should go for it!

You can't figure it out on your own without making mistakes and failing. You limit failures when you invest in winning from the start.

My mentors have played a crucial role in my professional development, and they still do. They've helped me make better decisions, largely because I can ask them insightful questions and know that I'm getting honest feedback based on their firsthand experience. My mentors have challenged my thinking and served as great professional contacts, introducing me to others who have helped me and opened up business opportunities that I probably wouldn't have otherwise found.

Today, I'm a mentor myself for several entrepreneurs and business owners. We meet regularly in support of their success. I guide them with a proven step-by-step plan for their business growth, giving them direction in areas they are unclear about. It requires deliberate and purposeful engagement with them to know how to best achieve success and to help them avoid unnecessary failure. Working alongside someone who has "been there and done that" many times over will shorten your learning curve and dramatically increase your success, especially when they are as committed to your growth as you are.

The number-one reason I wanted to support and mentor others once I had achieved my own success was that mentoring changed my life in every industry I've invested in. I learned from successful people already making it out there in the world. They were the best at what they did and taught me how to avoid as much failure as possible to survive in business. I could never have done it all on my own, and I certainly didn't learn how to avoid failure in school. I had to learn it on my own, one failure at a time.

I DIDN'T LEARN ABOUT FAILURE IN SCHOOL

Schools may teach knowledge, but life requires wisdom to survive. Wisdom means knowing what to do when things go wrong. But instead of learning critical life skills about how to deal with failure, stress, finances, and business in general, most people are taught to memorize information. This is somewhat helpful, but not at the cost of learning critical life skills.

Some people learn life skills from parents, but not all parents are equipped to teach these lessons. Some parents assume the child got enough from school to get by in the world.

Even college claims to be the safe, sure way to find a successful career. But it's not. Whether or not you went to college, and whether or not you want to work for yourself or for a company, building skills and experience in a desired field is what brings results. Don't expect schooling to get you anywhere unless you have the work experience and life skills to go with it.

In school, you get graded, but those grades can distort your perception of reality. Maybe you got straight A's in school, but in the real world you have no common business sense.

I DIDN'T LEARN ABOUT FAILURE IN SCHOOL, continued

And if you don't have good business sense, you can get a lot of F's for failing in business and in life.

Common business sense is not taught in schools, yet it has allowed me to survive and thrive most of my life. I learned it by paying attention to what does and doesn't work firsthand from my grass-roots business experience.

I consider my good common business sense a gift. It gave me a keen understanding of what to do in most business situations. It taught me to make good decisions and avoid many failures. And best of all, it taught me to pay close attention to reality!

School teaches that effort brings a measurable, predictable, and successful result. The real world doesn't work like that. If you get an A for effort in school, you succeed every time. If you get an A for effort in life, you're lucky to succeed after numerous tries.

For example, Stephen King, one of the bestselling authors in the world, failed dozens of times when he was starting out. His first book, *Carrie*, was rejected by 30 publishers, one of whom predicted that the book would never sell. After so many rejections, King threw the manuscript in the trash. Luckily, his wife retrieved it and urged him to give it another try. *Carrie* finally sold, and the book and subsequent movie received an A+ in the business world.

Colonel Harland Sanders reportedly received 1,009 rejections (or F's) while trying to sell his franchise-model chicken restaurant before getting his first A. He sold his idea to an existing restaurant, which became the first Kentucky Fried Chicken. Those "secret herbs and spices" tripled the restaurant's sales in the first year.

Walt Disney was fired from a newspaper as a young man because his editor gave him an F, stating Disney "lacked imagination and had no good ideas." He went on to receive many A's in life, including 59 Academy Award nominations and 22 wins, as one of the most creative animators of all time.

If school is meant to prepare people for success, then why is it absolutely failing to accomplish this? In school you're taught to memorize something to get good grades. Yet in business, how does memorizing facts allow you to avoid failure?

> **I DIDN'T LEARN ABOUT FAILURE IN SCHOOL,** continued
>
> School doesn't teach you how to deal with failure. And making mistakes will become a natural and necessary part of your success equation.

Focus on Course Correction

You will make mistakes, but don't get defeated. You can only make mistakes if you are staying in motion and trying new things. If something doesn't work out, you can always course correct and try something else.

You can learn valuable lessons from your mistakes when you pay close attention. Some mistakes actually lead to wonderful new opportunities. But if you aim too low because you're worried about making mistakes, it could actually lead to much bigger errors in business (and life).

Most people aim low in life because of low self-esteem. As a result, they don't strive for something bigger due to fear of failure. Once you aim low, your level of success is capped, your motivation drops, and you start thinking and playing small. On the other hand, people who aim high for big goals will always gain more and have more success.

A good example of how someone turned failures into massive success is professional boxer George Foreman. He left his successful boxing career to become a minister in 1980 after a personal religious experience in the locker room. His ministry struggled, however, and by 1987 his youth center was near bankruptcy. Foreman decided to go back into boxing, even though he was considered far too old at this point. But he ignored his doomsayers and made his comeback.

At age 45, Foreman became the oldest heavyweight boxing champion in the world when he defeated 26-year-old Michael Moorer in a 1994 bout. He finally retired from boxing five years later. Outside the ring, Foreman has since become enormously wealthy as an entrepreneur and TV pitchman for a variety of products, including the hugely popular George Foreman Grill. He has also continued to preach and run his youth center. Just as Foreman maximized the value of his mistakes and converted them into successes, you can do the same by being a lifelong student from failure.

Become a Lifelong Student of Failure

Some people think that all you have to do to succeed is get to the point where you're smart enough to no longer fail. That belief is simply not realistic. As your business grows, you must always continue to try new things, and you won't always succeed the first time around.

Recognize that setbacks happen all the time as part of the learning process. The most successful people are able to "fail forward"—fail in such a way as to gain valuable insights that lead to more successful outcomes the next time. You must be able to hold yourself accountable for the failure, dust yourself off, and turn things around.

Using this process can set you up for a continuous cycle of success. When you train your mind to achieve, you make success the norm. When you quit sabotaging yourself, you also:

- quit whining about what's not working;
- quit beating yourself up when things don't go right;
- quit exaggerating your losses; and
- quit taking failures personally.

Separate the failure from yourself. Taking failure personally can damage your self-esteem and drive your belief system into a downward spiral.

Move away from failure by reevaluating, refocusing, and redirecting your actions!

As I write this, I'm reminded of some real-life stories from successful business owners who experienced small failures or a slump in business. Although these failures were certainly not large enough to put them out of business, they seemed devastating at the time. One client complained to me, "This is the worst year of my life! Business is a disaster!" In reality, the business was only down 20 percent.

Once I evaluated the reasons behind the loss, it was clear that their lack of implementing new ideas was one of the keys to the downturn. Another reason for the income loss was that they had stopped using the proven marketing efforts that had worked in the past to bring in most of their new clients.

This profit downturn was simply a slump they could turn around quickly by developing a strategic monthly action plan with a stronger commitment to including a few new business strategies. The process began by implementing the easiest strategies first to create quick results. This was done in the form of securing more income from existing customers. I also suggested that they bring back their proven marketing strategies, rather than trying new marketing ideas that could take time to develop.

Another successful business owner shared a "slump story" with me by saying, "We are just not on our game, and we don't know why." In fact, sales were down because their sales offer changed, and they had raised their prices at the same time. This had worked in the past, but the outcome had changed—not once, but twice. My suggestion was to analyze their every move since they made that very first successful sales offer. Then they just needed to go back to a price point that worked in the past to generate more-consistent income.

Lesson learned: If it isn't broken, don't fix it!

Lessons I Learned from One of My Biggest Failures

All this talk about failure reminds me of my biggest failure in my speaking business, when my lack of motivation to market my business nearly dried up all my opportunities. I quit doing the marketing that had been successful for years. Why?

At the time, I was in a business partnership traveling around the world. Much of the time it was exciting to discover the world together—until the partnership became unbalanced. I believed I was doing most of the work, and I was getting tired of the heavy travel schedule.

I think now that I subconsciously self-sabotaged my income opportunities by not marketing the business properly. The business opportunities began to drop off, and the partnership failed. In retrospect, this is exactly what I wanted (even if I didn't realize it at the time). Here are the five key lessons I learned from my mistakes in this situation:

1. *Don't put all your eggs in one business basket.* I ignored my existing business and put 100 percent of my focus and energy into the new business. When the partnership failed, I had to rebuild, reinvent, and refocus my marketing efforts back into my individual business. My income dropped until I built a new brand and a strong foundation for my company to take off again.

2. *Don't ignore the obvious.* My business partner knew how to sell from the stage. I wanted to learn this skill and believed she was the perfect person to teach me, so I asked to hire her to teach me sales skills. She responded, "I would rather go into business with you and partner up because you have marketing and business skills I need to learn." The conversation quickly turned from learning from each other into a business partnership where we ignored the obvious: We had different core business values.

3. *Don't allow emotions to fog judgment.* We both got caught up in the excitement of developing a world speaking tour. Our energies were focused on getting booked to speak rather than on developing a more strategic business plan. Our excitement and emotions overrode our logic. Sometimes good ideas can go bad fast. Most ideas that crash and burn originate from a positive and genuine place, but along the way things go awry. To avoid this pitfall, remove emotions when making a big business decision.

4. *Balance workload and commitment evenly.* Although the business partnership started out with balanced task assignments,

the workload ended up shifting in my direction. At the time it seemed logical since I had stronger marketing and people skills. I created most of the international connections and got most of the speaking engagements. But I eventually realized I didn't need a partner to just show up after I did most of the work developing and marketing the business.

5. *Make sure the partnership works for the long haul.* In hindsight, I should have taken more time to discuss long-term business strategy. Instead, I jumped in with both feet and started to work without knowing where it would lead. I learned to stop making rash business decisions and to not to make demands of someone who doesn't have the skills to back it up. It was unfair for me to expect my partner to react the same way I would. This set us both up for unrealistic expectations from the start. But in the long run, this business failure allowed me to define a new meaning of success. I discovered I wanted to create a new business model with a more independent, financially free lifestyle. This also allowed me to refocus my business back to the United States.

Once I stopped holding on to what wasn't working in my business and walked away, a new opportunity walked in. As I was going through a challenging time folding up the partnership, I met the love of my life.

My husband, Greg, was the new partner who could sustain a lifetime of love and support beyond anything I could have ever dreamed. As I reinvented my business, we also built a new life together. My business thrived and my income tripled within two years.

Not All Failures Are as Dramatic as They Appear

My business partnership was successful for a few years before it ran its course. With every failure, I learned to take responsibility for the lessons and appreciate the benefits that came with them: knowledge, new skills, personal growth, and opportunity.

You don't need to think of every mistake as a huge failure. Most people have a tendency to magnify the potential crisis that a failure may bring. Others use their imagination to make a failure appear larger or more dramatic than it actually is.

Failure usually creates opportunities for new resources, new information, and new people to flow to you. Pay close attention to what changes may have caused a failure to happen. Define what has changed to cause the failure or the slump, and then be ready to accept the change.

One way you can do that is to journal your thoughts every time there is a failure or slump—to analyze what happened, so emotions don't fog your judgment. Learn how to turn things around by gaining clarity. Here are some questions you can ask to help analyze any failure situation:

- Have you stopped trying new ideas or strategies that could create more income-generating results? If so, why?
- Have you or your team failed to remain motivated to implement new ideas? If so, why?
- Have you changed or eliminated an area of marketing that could bring in new customers? If so, why?
- Have you made a change in your sales or service offering that may have slowed down income? If so, why?
- Has a business partnership become unbalanced and ineffective? If so, why?
- Have you self-sabotaged success opportunities, causing a failure in any way? If so, why? How did sabotaging your opportunities play out, and what have you learned that will help you avoid this in the future?

If you're in a "failure phase" right now, take some time to answer these questions and really reflect on what your answers mean. You might be surprised by the results! No matter what level of success you have, failures big and small will continue to test you. These tests will help you become stronger and smarter all the time. It's how you choose to deal with failure that makes all the difference in your success.

You must be willing to make a few mistakes and suffer a little pain to get what you want. Don't sell yourself short!

All that said, this is the most important thing to remember, reinforce, and focus on: It doesn't matter how many times you failed in the past; what matters are the times you succeeded. Use failures, slumps, and mistakes as a way to learn and then dismiss the negativity. Hold a picture of past successes in mind because everyone has succeeded at something. When beginning a new task, call up the feelings you experienced during some past success, however small it was. Choose to focus on the success, not the possibility of failure. Then focus on the solution, not the problem.

When you focus on a problem, it's easy to give up, cut back, stop taking chances, and reduce your energies from trying to figure out why things aren't working. Another reason it's often easier to see problems instead of solutions is because you don't feel worthy of being, doing, or having what you desire.

You can only attract what you feel worthy of. The greater your feelings of self-worth, the more you value yourself, and the more risk you are willing to take to better yourself and your business.

IF YOU REFUSE TO BE GUIDED BY LESSONS, FAILURE WILL GUIDE YOU

When I sold my first two retail stores, the new owners gained instant access to a very successful company with a loyal following, proven brand, and working systems in place, which is why people buy successful companies or franchises in the first place.

IF YOU REFUSE, continued

The new owners also gained access to amazing retail mentors through a low-cost monthly networking event, which was held to support one another with innovative marketing strategies and new ideas for business growth. This powerful group had decades of experience in the retail industry and were known as the best-of-the-best retailers in the Chicago area.

These retailers had been my mentors and taught me so much about the business. In fact, their advice and guidance helped me grow my first small retail store into multiple locations and a multimillion-dollar business within a few short years. For this reason, I was extremely excited to share the group with the new owners.

But both new owners stopped attending the monthly mentoring meetings shortly after purchase. This completely shocked me. When I asked why, their answers shocked me even more.

One said she feared public speaking, so she avoided the meetings because she didn't want to speak in front of the small group. The other new owner said, "Well, it interferes with my bowling night."

How crazy is that? Bowling is more important than learning how to run a new business?

More bad business decisions followed, and the writing was on the wall. Within a couple of years, both had failed.

Success could have been so easy. It was all planned out, the guides were available, but each one chose to follow a much more challenging path all alone while making bad mistakes based on poor judgment. Their failures caused the doors on the business to close forever.

It was simple common business sense. All they had to do was follow the successful plan already laid out and take action on what was proved to work.

Be Willing to Do Things You Don't Want to Do

How you react to obstacles and challenges will define your level of success. Avoidance is a hard habit to break. The more you avoid what you don't think you are good at or are uncomfortable with, the harder it is to face challenges head-on.

To succeed, you must be willing to do the things no one else wants to do. The things that frustrate you. The things about which you say, "It won't work," "I'm afraid of . . . ," or "I don't have time for . . ."

Here are seven things you can do (even if you don't want to!) to avoid failure:

1. Take responsibility for failures and move on.
2. Try again even though everything up to now has been a failure.
3. Don't take mistakes and failures personally.
4. Analyze problems, find solutions, and make decisions.
5. Refuse to quit, no matter what obstacles get in the way.
6. Turn mistakes into lessons to shift in a new direction.
7. Deliver results instead of making excuses for what didn't work.

Everyone hates to fail. Many people, maybe including yourself, hate failing so much that they give up trying—after all, if you don't try, you can't fail, and if you don't fail, you don't have to deal with the negative emotions connected to failure. But this gets you nowhere except to say at least you haven't failed at anything. How boring would that be? And avoiding failure altogether will get you nowhere in life.

Hang in there through your failures. If you pay attention they will teach you a lot. And once you're on the other side of failure, you will have learned how to avoid more of them in the future. And best of all, you will begin to build your confidence and continue to survive, succeed, and thrive.

Practice Overcoming Failure with the Best-Case and Worst-Case Scenarios

A lot of people tend to assume the worst-case scenario when taking on a new risk or challenge. They prepare themselves for the worst possible outcome, which is often viewed as a survival instinct. The problem with this is that some people remain stuck in the worst-case scenario mindset for too long. When this happens they tend to view obstacles from a victim mindset vs. a solution-oriented mindset, and they come from a defensive point of view vs. an offensive viewpoint. And they can even make matters worse when they share their worst case viewpoint with others, making it appear that this is the only inevitable outcome.

To overcome the fear of failure, you must be willing to face it before you start by asking, "What is the worst that can happen?" But don't stay stuck there. Then prepare mentally for the worst-case scenario. This builds your confidence so you can handle even the greatest challenges.

The essence of realistic thinking is examining the worst-case scenario in your mind first. The goal isn't to be negative or assume the worst, but to prepare in case it does happen. Most of the time the worst never happens. But, by chance it does, you are ready to overcome it. This way, you give yourself the best chance possible for better results.

When you prepare for the worst and develop contingency plans to meet it, you become more confident and secure. It's reassuring to know that surprises are unlikely.

Disappointment is the difference between expectations and reality. Realistic thinking minimizes the difference between the two —instead of remaining stuck. Therefore, if you picture the worst-case scenario and examine it honestly, you give yourself a reality check for just about anything that can happen. It's as if you are practicing how to deal with failure before it possibly exists.

To perform well in a crisis, learn certain life skills that allow you to react positively when under pressure. Learn to react to a crisis with a productive mindset to find a solution. If you have played out the worst-case scenarios in your mind first, you are ready to take on anything.

Don't forget to also consider the best case scenario, the reason you are considering the risk, change or obstacle in the first place. Consider viewing the situation from the standpoint that it is inevitable that the outcome will be successful—as you want it to be. This allows you to begin preparing for a successful outcome.

For example, let's say someone is facing a situation where money is tight in their business, but they have an idea to launch a new service or offer and there is no guarantee that their clients will invest in their new service or offer. They will also need to invest a large amount of marketing dollars to give the new launch a try. And so they say, "I'll do my best, and I'm not going to worry about it. I'll keep investing my marketing dollars until the money runs out." First of all it sounds empowering that they are willing to go for it and give it a try since that's the way marketing often works—with trial and error. But the "running of of money" part of this statement is a killer. This viewpoint is coming from a victim mentality that has emotionally decided that "running out of money" is an option. Worse yet, they perceive it as an option that is beyond their control. This means they believe it has more power over them than they have power over it. And once they allow this option as the only way, they begin to prepare for it as the inevitable.

On the other hand, they could say, "This is just not being realistic. Maybe I need to add some common business sense into the mix along with the best-case scenario."

One could just as easily say, "I'm going to do my best, and be realistic with my marketing spending and evaluate this situation from the most creative and insightful manner I can. So I'll do whatever I can to create a best case situation where I earn more income from making this offer. After all, that's why I'm going for it. Running out of money and not having cash flow in my business is simply not an option. Therefore, it's not worth my worry because I will not let that situation happen."

Can you see the big difference between the two completely different viewpoints or scenarios?

When you always assume success, you plan for the best-case scenario and realistically prepare yourself for the worst-case scenario so that you can do everything in your power to prepare for success.

Shameless, No-Nonsense Action Steps and Affirmation

Success Is Easy Affirmation (say it, believe it, and own it): "Success comes easy to me because I turn my failures into lessons for personal and professional growth."

1. *Take complete ownership of your failures.* When you learn how to admit and accept your failures, life and success become easier. If you don't learn from your mistakes, you will keep repeating the same bad business habits. Recognize that failure is placed in front of us all to teach us lessons and help direct our actions in a new direction.

2. *Surround yourself with can-do people who find solutions in problems, instead of those who think things can't get done.* Successful people play the game to win even when they fail. Unsuccessful people play not to lose. After all, you are a winner!

3. *Turn your mistakes into lessons.* Don't get defeated. Most mistakes will smooth out in time as you continue to move in a new direction. When you are willing to move beyond failure, success will become easier. Learn how to not fear things that appear challenging by sharpening your willpower and bridging the gap between where you are and where you want to be. Refocus on a clearer and more direct way to achieving results, which is typically the easiest, smoothest, and most realistic path.

4. *Don't allow emotions to get in the way of making good common-sense business decisions.* Failures are there to help you become stronger, smarter, and more successful. You will learn valuable lessons from mistakes when you pay attention. Recognize that setbacks happen all the time as part of life and the learning process. The most successful people can "fail forward" in such a way as to gain valuable insight that will lead to more successful outcomes the next time. Hold yourself accountable for the failure, pick yourself up, dust yourself off, and turn things around.

5. *Practice overcoming failure with best-case and worst-case scenarios to help you make decisions more effectively.* To overcome the fear of failure, be willing to face it before starting an endeavor by asking yourself, "What is the worst that can happen?" Next, prepare mentally for the worst-case and

the best-case scenarios. This begins to build your confidence and enables you to handle challenges with ease. Reviewing possible scenarios allows you to examine the possibilities in your mind before taking action. The goal is to prepare you for just about anything that could happen in advance, giving you the greatest chance for possible best returns in your decision-making process.

shameless
self-promotion
and strategic
marketing

SUCCESS IS EASY . . .
with Shameless Self-Promotion

One of the most masterful self-promoters of all time was boxer Muhammad Ali. He was well-known for tooting his own horn: "I am the greatest. I said that even before I knew I was."

This isn't bragging if you can back it up like Ali did. Ali was one of the first sports stars and TV personalities to make shameless self-promotion an art form. At the time, Ali shocked the world with his outrageous self-promoting claims such as, "I am the greatest!" He kept repeating it so that it would become how people remembered him.

He used the power of novelty and repetition to create other people's perceptions as he built his personal brand. He became known to the world as The Greatest.

Ali believed so strongly in his goal of becoming THE boxing champion that he shared it out loud for the world to hear in the form of an affirmation, a positive statement asserting that a goal you want to achieve is already happening (just like the affirmations you see at the end of each chapter).

When sharing an affirmative statement with someone else, the point is to either believe it is already true or strongly believe it will come true. When telling someone about a goal, it pushes you toward achieving the goal so as not to disappoint. That is why sharing goals in the form of an affirmation motivates a person to reach goals sooner.

Before every fight, Ali prepared by training both his body and his mind. He had such a strong belief in his abilities that he dared to announce it to the world. By repeating his affirmations again and again, Ali was training his subconscious to support his victory. He also set up his competition to lose by repeating statements such as, "Float like a butterfly, sting like a bee," and "Not only do I knock 'em out, I pick the round." Ali is an example of someone having the courage to become a fighter that achieves success and accepts nothing less. He shows that you can promote yourself by recognizing that you have greatness within yourself.

Ali trained for success through repeated visualization and affirmation. He stood out. He always spoke his mind and was never shy. This outlook came from his instilled beliefs and self-confidence. He talked so big that it forced him to succeed or lose face. Most important, he never gave up!

In this chapter, you will discover how to stand out and get noticed with shameless self-promotion. There is a big difference between ineffective and effective self-promotion. Ineffective self-promotion serves the person doing the promoting first; effective self-promotion serves *others* first. To succeed, you need to concentrate on effective self-promotion.

If You Don't Believe in Yourself, No One Else Will

Self-confidence is a key component of a successful self-promoter. Self-confidence allows you to accept your real self and provides momentum to put that authentic self out into the world for all to see. That's how you get noticed! What's the point of being the best at something if no one else knows about it?

Self-promotion is not bragging. Think of it instead as sharing the impact of your work with others. When you have something to share, you should be excited about it. Get so excited that other people want to be a part of it. People naturally gravitate to those who promote their business with passion and enthusiasm.

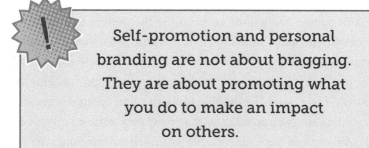

Self-promotion and personal branding are not about bragging. They are about promoting what you do to make an impact on others.

Don't allow the voices and opinions of other people to drown out the "inner voice" each of us has. Instead: Speak Up! We all need to have the courage to share our opinions and promote our gifts. It is important to remain true to yourself at all times. When you promote your knowledge, skills, and ideas, you give others something to cheer for. You give them a cause to support and follow.

Promote the things that make others feel good. Your accomplishments aren't likely to make other people feel good, but your ideas will. When you are inspired by actions or ideas, they will be inspired, too.

To gain recognition for your ideas, make sure your vision is as clear and concise as possible. Don't be afraid to share your thoughts and spread the message to everyone who can receive support in return.

Keep in mind it's not about you—it's about what you can do in the service of others.

Speak up! Speaking up and speaking out may cause some people to prejudge you. Some may instantly label you as overconfident or boastful. But people are going to decide whether to like you or not, and not everyone is going to like you, so don't bother trying to make them. Speaking your mind and standing up for what you believe in should never be compromised! Success is easy for people to notice when you have a strong vision and are willing to speak up. Don't let your fear of being disliked stand in the way of getting the word out.

Resenting Self-Promotion Will Sabotage Your Success

Successful people are willing to promote themselves and their value. Unsuccessful people think negatively about selling and promoting. Resenting self-promotion will become a huge obstacle to success!

People who have issues with selling and promotion aren't successful. The reason is obvious. How can you create success if you aren't willing to let people know that your products or services exist?

If you are not yet comfortable with self-promotion, there may be a number of reasons why. You may have had a bad experience in the past with other people's "shameful" self-promotion. Maybe they were giving you a hard sell or trying to get a sale at an inappropriate time. Maybe they just wouldn't take "no" for an answer. This can be frustrating and even piss you off! And it should! This is self-serving! These people were not promoting their ideas effectively, and because of this, they came across as pushy, rude, or intrusive. But remember—this doesn't happen when you promote skillfully, effectively, and in the service of others.

Another reason you may not feel comfortable with self-promotion is that you may have tried selling to someone who rejected you. We all hate rejection, but you need to get over it. No one I know has ever died from rejection. But, if you try to avoid rejection, it kills your business opportunities for growth. And that alone kills your chances for success!

Being rejected may cause you to develop an instant dislike for self-promotion. Yet, in this case, it's not self-promoting tha is causing your discomfort—it's the fear of rejection. To keep the fear from setting in, realize that the past does not have to repeat itself. Continued rejection is unlikely when you understand how to promote your products or services effectively. You can also train yourself to understand that rejection happens every day in business, sales, and promotion. You will win some and lose some. That's just the way it works.

Another issue around self-promotion may come from your past programming and beliefs. When growing up, some people are told it is not polite to talk about yourself or to "toot your own horn." But in the real world, if you don't toot your horn, no one else will.

If you don't toot your own horn, you can't enjoy the music.

What were your parents, teachers, or guardians like growing up? Did they believe in self-promotion? Expressing your personal beliefs and speaking your mind?

We may not like to admit it, but we are all creatures of habit, especially when those habits and beliefs have been programmed into our minds since childhood. We all have years of false, limiting beliefs rattling around in our heads that we battle every day.

Some people feel that self-promotion is beneath them. They probably also believe that if someone wants your products or services, somehow that person will find you. If this is your current mindset, get over it fast. It is a success killer. Believing this way will cost you endless lost opportunities, sabotage success, and drive your business into the ground. Business doesn't work this way!

Hoping that people will discover your business by chance in an overcrowded marketplace is a fantasy! No one will notice your business unless you make it easy for customers to find it and encourage them to spend money there.

It's important to figure out what experiences from the past are holding you back from promoting yourself. They are also keeping you from success!

Beliefs and Values Around Self-Promotion

The critical point here isn't whether you like to promote yourself. It all boils down to your beliefs and personal values. Ask yourself these questions:

- Do you believe in the product or service your business is offering?
- Do you believe what is offered will benefit the person it is promoted to?

If both answers are "yes," then you believe in the overall value of your business. So how is it appropriate to hide it from people who need your products or services?

More often than not, people who have a problem with self-promotion don't believe in the business and/or the products. Consequently, they have a hard time imagining other people believing in the value either. If you believe what you have to offer can help others, it's your duty to let as many people as possible know about it.

Why Believe Differently?

Some people have closed their minds against self-promotion, no matter how much it might benefit their business. Now, I don't expect a change in your beliefs overnight, but you can start by opening your mind to believing differently about self-promotion from this day forward.

There can be no true success if you aren't willing to let people know your business, products, or services exist. Choosing to become a successful self-promoter requires working to create more positive experiences and better results. The good news is that you can make the choice to change your beliefs and create a new reality starting right now.

Ineffective Self-Promotion vs. Effective Self-Promotion

There's a huge difference between ineffective self-promotion and effective self-promotion. Ineffective self-promotion serves the person doing the promoting first. Effective self-promotion serves others first.

One will sabotage success; the other moves everyone toward success.

Shameful self-promotion is ineffective promotion. Bragging about yourself is self-serving and a poor way to make positive connections with others. In fact, it's downright annoying! Excessively proud and boastful talk about your achievements or possessions turns people off. This type of self-promotion is not what I'm talking about in this chapter.

Shameless self-promotion succeeds because it comes from a much different place. When done effectively, self-promotion is an art form. It comes from a place of service. It comes from the passion and commitment to support others first. Effective self-promotion is natural when your words and actions connect your head and heart. When promoting effectively, more prospects are readily open to doing business. Simply put, effective self-promotion is good marketing!

Is being shameless a bad thing? No, not unless it's bad to believe in something so much you want to tell everyone you meet about it. Not unless it's bad to have such passion for what you do that you believe you are doing your prospects a disservice if you don't get out there and promote yourself.

Here is what the word "shameless" means to me: looking for opportunities everywhere to promote myself in the service of others. Does that sound self-serving, pushy, or intrusive? No! Serving others well is what success is all about! The reality is that if you don't do shameless promotion, you'll end up with nameless promotion.

Once you master the skill of effective self-promotion, it becomes easy to succeed at anything you set your mind to. In fact, when you promote yourself effectively, you reap further rewards by gaining followers. Having shameless fans who support your work means you are also adept at inspiring and motivating others to buy into your success vision.

Become Shamelessly Sold on Yourself

Before you can sell yourself to others, you must be sold on yourself. Your confidence, positive attitude, and enthusiasm will never fail you. Absolute assurance when promoting yourself is a must!

To become a shameless self-promoter, you must change your thinking from "What if . . . ?" to "What if I DON'T . . . ?" And if I don't, how much could I miss out on? A lot!

Selling yourself is about building trust. To sell is to serve.

You must find a way of selling that you can feel good about. Are you underselling because you fear being perceived as too pushy, too sales-y, too this, or too that? Learn how to ask for business so you can grow and expand. Some people say, "I just want to be happy," but that's a ridiculous cop-out for not promoting and selling!

You Cannot Not Market

In business, you understand that if you don't promote and market, you can't succeed. Right? No matter how great your service is or what amazing value you offer, if prospects don't know about you, you're not going to have a chance to do business with them.

To gain some clarity on this point, ask yourself the following questions:

- Do you feel passionate about helping prospects and customers get the best experience possible?
- Do you feel your services and/or products are better than your competitors'?
- Do you want to help others?

If the answer is "yes" to any of these questions, promote these facts. When you don't promote your services and products, you rob people of the opportunity to do business with someone who has the customer's best interest in mind.

Do you feel passionate about your business, career, and/or what you have to sell? I'm sure the answer is "yes," or why take the time to read this book?

When you passionately believe in yourself, your value, your service, and your products, you also believe prospects should do business with you instead of your competitors, right? If the answer is "no," I suggest finding your passion before going any further, or success will become challenging for you.

It's easy to promote yourself when you believe in the value of what you offer. To move to a higher level of success, you must practice promoting and selling in ways that may feel uncomfortable at first. Next time you experience a feeling of discomfort in self-promotion or the feeling of rejection creeps in, move toward it instead of away from it. Go ahead and feel uncomfortable. It is only a feeling. Step outside the limitation zone and go for it!

> Not promoting yourself goes against the grain of all sales and marketing success!

Learn to Never Give Up

Growing up in a family business, I learned early on that I had to self-promote on a daily basis if I wanted the business to succeed. Since my family had many different businesses, we were always promoting something new. Most of our businesses started out with little or no investment, so self-promotion was essential to getting them off the ground.

My father taught me that the first step toward marketing success was to believe in myself and my ideas. It doesn't matter if others don't believe in your ideas as much as you do, you must be strong enough to never give up!

Back in the mid-1970s, my father ran across a mini-storage business while traveling in Texas. It was a new concept at the time and intrigued him, so he stopped to inquire about it. The owner was very proud of his new business and openly shared the details of how he got started. My father then talked it over with the family, and we decided to start a mini-storage business in my home state of Indiana.

The next step was to get a bank loan to build the facility. That should have been simple, especially since our car rental business was already successful. But the banker wouldn't go for it. He said, "I've never heard of a mini-storage facility. It sounds like a fad to me. I don't think it will work."

One bank after another turned us down, but my father never gave up. Finally, we got approved for a small-business loan, although it was not quite enough to complete the entire project.

My father and brother jumped in to help the construction crew assemble the storage buildings to save money. As I ran the day-to-day car rental business, I started promoting the mini-storage concept to our existing customers. Before the project was even completed, we had a long waiting list of interested customers. As soon as the storage units became available, every space was rented.

Finally, the bank started believing in our business and offered to fund a second location. Within a few years we sold our successful

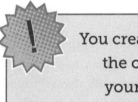

You create your own luck through the opportunities that come your way. Everyone has the opportunity to be lucky as long as they don't give up!

company to a large self-storage corporation, Public Storage. This experience taught me to always believe in my ideas, to promote them to the right people, and to never give up!

SHAMELESS SELF-PROMOTION AND HOWARD STERN

When my book *Confessions of Shameless Self-Promoters* was published, I was asked to be a guest on a lot of radio shows to share my shameless marketing tips. One day I picked up the phone and the person on the other end said, "This is K.C. Armstrong [a producer] from *The Howard Stern Show*. We heard about your book and want you to be a guest on the show. Are you interested?"

At first I thought, *Is this one of my friends playing a joke on me?*

But playing along, I said, "Howard is going to beat me up!"

The producer responded, "Oh, noooo!"

Part of me really wanted to believe him, but I knew better. This was shock jock Howard Stern. It was not going to be Howard and I having a nice casual business interview. Oh, noooo!

It was going to be three radio show hosts—whose job was to find something to make fun of or something outrageous to shock listeners—against one intimidated guest. The show really should be called *Get the Guest!*

But without even thinking, these words came flying out of my mouth: "Sure, I would love to be on Howard's show!"

What? Why would I agree? Mainly because I teach others to take bold action to shamelessly self-promote and to step outside the comfort or the limitation zone.

I needed to walk my talk. Even though this was way outside my own comfort zone, I needed to go for it!

The interview was going to be in a month, so I had time to seek out some supportive advice from business associates. I had earlier met Bill Goss at the National Speakers Convention who told me how he had been on *The Howard Stern Show* for more than an hour talking about

---

SHAMELESS SELF-PROMOTION, continued

his 30 near-death experiences. Yes, he nearly died 30 times! He even created a personal brand based on them: The Luckiest Unlucky Man Alive.

Bill was a successful keynote speaker who shared his life stories and the lessons learned from his accidents. He told me that when he was on the show, the other hosts ganged up on him and took the conversation in a more shocking and embarrassing direction, saying it was the most challenging interview of his life.

"Oh, great! I've already agreed to be on Howard's show! Now I have to find a way to survive it," I said to myself.

I asked Bill if he could coach me through different scenarios on just about every possible way the interview might go. Most were not pleasant.

Bill said, "You will probably only get about two minutes on the show before they hang up. They will cut you off if they can't find something outrageous, funny, or controversial to talk about. At best, you'll only want five minutes, no more. And that's only if you can handle the tough interview process."

I replied, "OK, I can do that! My goal is to get my five minutes of shameless fame keeping my clothes on (hey, it's radio) and my professionalism intact."

I can't say I respect everything about Howard Stern, but I do respect the fact that he is a successfully shameless self-promoter and a shamelessly successful survivor! He lives by The Three Rules of Shameless Success:

- *Shameless Rule #1*: Have your own personal style. Dare to be different!

- *Shameless Rule #2*: Never give up even when other people don't believe in you and your ideas, or tell you you're crazy.

- *Shameless Rule #3*: Stand out and get noticed. Position yourself in front of the right people who will listen and pay attention.

On the day of the interview, I was prepared for just about anything. I held my ground and survived five full minutes! I even made Howard laugh, which inspired him to promote

---

> ### SHAMELESS SELF-PROMOTION, continued
>
> my book live on the air. Since he had told me he doesn't promote books during the interview.
>
> What happened next surprised and amazed: My book moved up to a bestseller rank within one hour. Wow! That's the power of the media and 10 million listeners. And I had no idea that Howard's listeners even read books! LOL!

Shameless, No-Nonsense Action Steps and Affirmation

Success Is Easy Affirmation (say it, believe it, and own it): "Success comes easy to me because I'm comfortable with and effective at shameless self-promotion."

1. *Accept that if you don't do shameless promotion, you'll end up with nameless promotion.* If you don't promote yourself, no one else will. It's challenging to succeed if you are not willing to let others know that your business, products, or services exist. Choosing to become a successful self-promoter requires working to create more positive experiences and seek better results. You can choose to change your beliefs and create a new reality starting right now.

2. *Promote yourself more often and always in the service of others.* When done effectively, self-promotion is an art form. It comes from a place of service. It comes from your passion and commitment to support others first. Effective self-promotion is natural when words and actions connect our head and heart. When you promote effectively, more prospects are readily open to doing business with you. Simply put, effective self-promotion is good marketing!

3. *Speak up and get noticed.* Don't allow the voices and opinions of others to drown out your true "inner voice." Summon the courage to share your opinions and promote your gifts. It is

important to remain true to yourself at all times. When you promote your knowledge, skills, and ideas, you give others something to cheer for and a cause to support and follow.

4. *Understand that resenting self-promotion will become a huge obstacle to your success!* People who have issues with selling and promoting rarely succeed. To excel in this area, you must become absolutely sold on yourself, your abilities, your products, your services. Before you can sell yourself to others, you must first be sold on you.

5. *Learn to live by The Three Rules of Shameless Success:*
   - *Rule #1:* Have your own personal style. Dare to be different!
   - *Rule #2:* Never give up even when others don't believe in you or your ideas.
   - *Rule #3:* Stand out. Position yourself in front of the right people to get noticed.

SUCCESS IS EASY ...
with "Your ASK in Gear"

There's an old saying: "If you don't ask, you don't get." This is certainly true when it comes to business. Your ability to ask directly relates to the level of success you are able to achieve!

Asking is the simplest, most efficient, and most rewarding action you can take when it comes to succeeding. I'm a big believer in the power of asking!

Asking expands your capacity to do amazing things. Asking has paid off for me in business many times over. In fact, this book might never have been published if I had not made a simple ask.

While attending the National Speakers Convention in Dallas, Texas, I went to a workshop called "How to Market a Bestselling Book," presented by Jeffrey Hayzlett. He talked about book marketing and mentioned working with his major book publisher. I already knew that Jeffrey's book was published with Entrepreneur Press because I had seen his book featured in *Entrepreneur* magazine. I think I was literally drooling as Jeffrey spoke about the publisher and his footprint in the business book space.

Wiping my mouth, I raised my hand and asked, "Jeffrey, first of all, congratulations on your book success. I've seen your book featured in *Entrepreneur* magazine. Every month when I pick up that magazine, I dream of how amazing it would feel to have my book featured in that publication. I've been an entrepreneur all my adult life, and it's my perfect target market. How do I get them to look at my book?"

He responded, "Send me an email, and I'll connect you to my direct contact there."

About five minutes later, he stopped his presentation and looked my way again. "Debbie, I mean it," he said. "Don't forget to send me that email so that I can get you connected with my publisher."

"Yes, no problem!" I replied. He certainly didn't need to remind me. In fact, I was probably still drooling!

The audience was full of other speakers and authors that day, but I was the only one who asked a question that got this type of response. This surprised me since I didn't know Jeffrey very well at the time. I simply asked a question. It didn't require a "yes" or "no" answer. My ask didn't require any special favor. I just asked the right person at the right time!

The results of my ask that day was nothing short of miraculous!

Within ten days, I had connected with Jeffrey's referral at Entrepreneur Press and set up a time to talk by phone. On our very first call, Jeffrey's contact told me she was excited about the book project and thrilled about the possibility of working with me.

It is rare for a major publisher to respond with interest so quickly. I've sold a few of my books to major publishers, but only through my New York book agent, and only after completing a very lengthy book proposal. Getting strong interest from a major publisher with only a title, a short description, and one phone call is almost unheard of!

After the book deal was agreed on and signed, I circled back around to ask Jeffrey if he would write the book's foreword. As you can see, he said yes.

Lesson learned: If you ask the right person at the right time, it can lead to life-changing results. In this chapter, you will learn how to do just that—ask for (and receive) what you most want with easy and achieve effective results, almost like magic.

Ask For What Others Won't

You can't afford to sit back and over analyze the details of your request or make excuses for why someone might say "no." The word "no" doesn't intimidate successful people. Success in business is tied to a willingness to ask for what others won't. Since successful people know how to ask respectfully, you will be respected. People will answer your questions and go the extra mile to help you because successful people want to support other successful people!

To get what you want, you need to learn to ask for it even when it might feel uncomfortable. Choosing success also means choosing to live a life of discomfort much of the time. You must do things that make you feel uncomfortable, especially when you believe the potential rewards are worthwhile.

For success to find you, don't waste time and energy worrying about what could go wrong. Focusing on the positive outcome may result in getting more than you expected.

Asking For Help Cultivates Success

While asking for help may appear challenging at times, it makes you stronger, more successful, and more confident. Asking is a brave act, especially when it's a big ask. When you learn to bravely ask without worrying about getting turned down, you may receive amazing

"DON'T MAKE ME COME OVER THERE AND KICK YOU IN THE ASK!"

Many people would rather make an ask for someone else than for themselves. It feels more comfortable asking on someone else's behalf because it's not a personal slight if you get a "no."

One of the biggest challenges in learning to ask for help is realizing that asking for your own sake does not mean you are selfish or trying to manipulate others. You are simply attempting to create an opportunity—often one that is a perfect win/win for everyone involved.

If you don't learn to ask early in your business career, excuses can pile up on you. And before you know it, you can't talk yourself into asking for anything. When this happens, I suggest you recognize your mental block around asking, and then work on removing it. That's probably a lot more pleasant than having me come over there and "kick you in the ask!"

One of my personal consulting clients turned around our working relationship by asking me if I would in turn invest in hiring her. My client, Arlene Gale (aka The Book Writing Business Coach) helps coach her clients through the book-writing process. But this was my ninth book, and I've never hired a book coach before. So why did I need her now?

Here are two reasons: First, because she asked me. Her ask allowed me to consider the possibility. Second, I was a bit stuck on where to get started with the book, and I knew it was going to be a long, lonely project. Working with a coach allowed me to brainstorm new ideas, gain instant feedback, and look outside my own perspective. After thinking about it, I realized it made perfect sense to hire her. And I'm thrilled that I said "yes" to working with Arlene. She helped me complete my book proposal quickly, and that got me an easy win from my publisher.

Arlene and I now share fun stories about how "getting her ask in gear" keeps paying off in growing her business. Anytime she doesn't feel comfortable asking someone for their business, she thinks of me as if I were sitting on her shoulder, saying, "Don't make me come over there and kick you in the ask!" Even when I'm not there, I help motivate her to get out of her own way and make a quick ask!

rewards. If you get a "no" even when you do everything right, that means you shouldn't take it personally.

Asking for help shows others you trust their ideas, believe in their competence, and respect their advice. You have the power to appreciate the value of the people you surround yourself with. Recognizing someone's value can come in the form of asking for help.

If you don't ask, you'll never know how much business and success you missed. For example, instead of asking for their business, you might wait for a potential client to get back to you because you don't want to appear too pushy. But what if that prospect assumes you're not interested in building a client relationship and gives their business to someone else? All because you didn't bother to follow up. People respect those who follow up.

Now let's walk through a few best practices for asking.

Ask Before the Window Closes

Often you have only a small window of time to ask your question, so you may only get one good shot at it. When this happens, you must be ready to make your ask before the window closes.

When is the best time to ask? Probably right now! Waiting for the "perfect moment" means you will probably never ask. Start out by asking easy questions. Make the request short and to the point. Pose simple, well-timed requests providing just enough information so the other person can best determine how to respond. Don't get bogged down in too many details.

Asking Is Simply Making a Choice

You can't know someone's answer to a question you haven't asked. So why try to figure it out beforehand and talk yourself out of asking? Deciding to ask is simply making a choice. When the ask is tied to your goal setting, you know where you want to go. You are just looking for guidance to support your decision.

Get to the point and keep the question brief. Successful people are good decision-makers. Most have limited time and a short attention span, so they appreciate it when you are equally decisive and get to the point quickly.

Don't be an Ask-Hole

An Ask-Hole is a person who asks for your opinion, yet never uses your advice. They often do the opposite of what you said to do. Ask-Holes sometimes ask questions for the sake of asking questions. They are big time wasters! Ask-Holes don't value your feedback or your response. They disappear into a dark hole because the asker ends up doing things the way he planned to all along. No one likes an Ask-Hole!

Ever have someone ask you, "Can I pick your brain?" Asking in this way is annoying and ineffective because the question is too general, self-serving, and often a waste of time.

Instead, give some context on why the ask is necessary. For example, "A mutual business associate said you would be a good resource to give me some helpful advice on . . ." Be sure to give more details on the specific topic, communicate clearly, and ask effectively. This way of asking comes across as more focused and respectful.

When you ask for someone's advice, find a way to put it into action fast. If you start making excuses about how the advice won't help or you create a negative thought around it, you won't take advantage of something that can turn into the perfect solution to a problem or challenge. By not following through, you will never know what is possible.

Be a Good Listener When Asking

You build better business connections and more meaningful conversations when you take the time to listen. Everyone wants to be heard. Listening also requires you to get comfortable with silence. Don't formulate your response before listening to the other person's answer.

People feel respected when you really listen. When you feel heard, you form better relationships and communication flows freely. Ask questions, explore the answers, and respond. Listen for both what is said and what isn't. Pay attention to body language.

Having a deeper awareness of your asking opportunities enhances your ability to make more appropriate requests. Pay attention so you know when to ask for more. Listen to what people are saying and notice when someone isn't saying anything.

This skill translates into other situations as well. When you master the art and skill of listening, you show powerful self-confidence, patience, support, and control. One of the best ways to become masterful at the ask is to become a good interviewer. Ask questions that will help you understand the other person's situation, and then concentrate on listening to her response.

When you allow the person you are asking (like a prospective customer) to do most of the talking, you can take notes on the comments. You also have time to think about how you will best respond—instead of interrupting with useless chatter. Listening allows you to remain focused and hear the unique problems or concerns of a prospect.

Your goal should be to get better at recognizing what questions you need to ask, of whom, and for what. When you master that, you'll find asking is easy. You can learn to become masterful by studying others who are already "masters of the ask." Pay close attention to how they bravely, respectfully, and powerfully make requests to create win/win opportunities.

Gain Instant Recognition with the Ask

Now let's talk about a few ways that mastering the art of the ask can help you grow your success.

For starters, if you aren't being heard or acknowledged in a meeting, raise your hand or stand up. This increases your voice power and energy. When you ask, make good eye contact and gestures to convey key points. Successful people ask questions often to understand what's going on and determine what their next action should be. You don't want to waste time going in the wrong direction.

Asking on the phone adds another dynamic to the conversation because you can't see the other person or read their body language. Therefore, gaining clarity is even more important. Even timing phone calls can be a challenge—be sure to ask if it's a good time to talk. But be aware that giving the other person an opt-out like that may also lead to a missed opportunity. Get more direct in asking without a closed-ended response.

While on the phone, honor each side of the conversation and plan to wrap up the call at the agreed-on time. Keeping to a time limit shows respect for the other person and leaves the door open to making future requests.

Ask for More Business

Most people don't feel comfortable asking for more business from existing clients, because asking is intimidating. But not asking for more business from customers who already trust and value your services is very costly because it's easier to get repeat business from existing customers than it is to chase after new prospects. Think about what other products or services you could offer to your customers and ask for more business.

When your customers enjoy doing business with you, you will get more referrals to their friends, family, and business associates. To gain more customer referrals, ask. It should be easy to ask for a referral after you've delivered great service. Asking doesn't mean you are taking advantage of your customer; it means you are supporting the customer's success or happiness. You can reward customers for referring others—by creating a customer referral reward program, for example. Offer a cash back or gift reward for an direct customer referrals.

Or, perhaps customers compliment you on your business or service. That is the perfect time to ask for a personal testimonial. For example, respond to the compliment with, "Thank you so much. A wonderful compliment like that could help more people like you get the same great value. Would you mind if I shared your compliment in the form of a testimonial?"

Most people will gladly agree to share. Next, put the testimonial in writing—or, better yet, pull out your phone and ask to record it on video. Video testimonials are even more powerful than written ones when used in online marketing.

Ask for the Sale

One of the most challenging ways of asking for business is asking for the sale. Too many people are afraid of this. If this sounds like you, learn to get over it fast!

Not asking people to invest with you and your services will keep you poor. To succeed at anything, learn how to ask for the sale.

One of the best ways to get better at this is to start investing in yourself first. Think about it. How can you expect someone to invest in you if you aren't willing to invest in yourself? For example, before I could feel comfortable asking someone to make a big investment in my business consulting services, I had to make a big investment in myself.

After making my first $20,000 investment in my business education, I felt even stronger about the value I had to offer. I believed what I offered was worth much more than what I had invested in. But investing that money is what got me to think differently in the first place. It made a huge boost in my confidence and made me more comfortable asking others to invest in me. Business started flowing to me much more easily. I raised my fees and started to ask for the sale more often. This dramatically increased my sales success and my income.

Another way to get more comfortable asking for the sale is to start asking smarter, more meaningful questions. Ask open-ended questions and listen closely to how your prospects answer. Consider what they need and want the most.

Keep in mind what's most important for them when deciding to invest. Use follow-up questions to clarify their needs, such as, "Would you please tell me more about . . .?" or "How will that work best for you?" When it comes to asking for money, you need to get more direct with your questions, such as, "How would you like to move forward?" or "Which one would you like to invest in?"

People don't like to be sold to, but they do want to invest in people who give them great value and ask questions that matter to them. Asking the right questions in advance will always help close more sales.

Never meet a prospect cold. Always ask prospects to give answers to focused questions before you talk in person or by phone. This gives you time to do some research in advance, which helps you stay on point and saves time. Then schedule a specific amount of time for the meeting or call. Once the prospect is supported with advice for approximately 20 to 30 minutes, you can feel comfortable asking for the sale. For example, ask the prospects to complete a pre-call questionnaire. It's easy to create question-and-answer forms with an online service like JotForm, Doodle, or Google Forms.

If you've done a good job asking the right questions and staying on point, it should be an easy ask. Being prepared will also prevent wasting time with "tire-kickers" who just want to take advantage of free advice.

When it comes to asking for the sale, one size doesn't fit all. Although they often elicit similar responses, you're dealing with different people who may communicate differently. This is why asking for the sale is a learned skill—and somewhat of an art form.

When communicating with prospects, be sure to pay close attention to what is and isn't working in the conversation. When you

Don't take "no" for an answer. You either have the wrong prospect, or you need to ask for more information.

observe the prospect's reactions and your own, you'll begin to learn how to better ask for the sale. Always ask your prospect if it's okay with them to record the phone call so that you can capture all of the information discussed on the call. You can only record the call if they agree in advance. If you do record it, be sure to play it back and review the conversation so that you can continue to improve.

Shameless, No-Nonsense Action Steps and Affirmation

Success Is Easy Affirmation (say it, believe it, and own it): "Success comes easy to me because I have the skill of asking for what I want and need."

1. *Ask even when it might feel uncomfortable.* When you continue to ask, you will create some life-changing, successful results. Asking is the simplest, most efficient, and most rewarding action you can take when it comes to achieving success. Asking expands your capacity to do amazing things.

2. *Ask respectfully.* Appreciate the value of the people you surround yourself with, and don't become an Ask-Hole. Asking for help shows others you trust their concepts and believe in their competence, especially when you take action to implement the ideas that are shared.

3. *Decide to make asking a new success habit.* Deciding to ask is making a choice. When your ask is tied to goal setting, you're simply asking for guidance to support your success. Learn to become confident enough to stand alone, smart enough to know when you need help, and brave enough to ask for it.

4. *Ask for more business.* When customers enjoy doing business with you, it's natural for them to want to refer friends, family, and business associates. Ask for referrals for services or products. You can't afford to sit back and over-analyze the details of your ask or make excuses why they might say "no." While asking for help may appear challenging at times, it will also make you stronger, more successful, and more confident.

Asking is a brave act, especially when it's a big ask. When you learn to ask bravely without worrying about getting turned down, it may result in amazing rewards.

5. *Ask for the sale.* Getting comfortable with directly asking for the sale at the right time will help you close more sales and create more income. Not asking people to invest with you and your services will keep you from achieving the success you deserve. To succeed at anything, you must learn how to ask for the sale. Don't make me come over there and "kick you in the ask!"

SUCCESS IS EASY . . .
with the Right Mix
of Skills and Traits

A chieving success is like following a recipe. When you use the right ingredients, it produces delicious results. But even with a good recipe, there are still bad cooks. Why is that? Because they don't follow the recipe with the right ingredients and focused dedication. They also don't get the proper guidance or don't have the talent or skills to execute properly. So when they stray from even the simplest recipes, the results can range from mediocre to catastrophic.

Good cooks, on the other hand, know how to mix and prepare the right ingredients to perfection. They combine the ingredients with the instructions, which makes for a combination of success. When you execute a well-balanced business recipe, success is easier and results are better.

It doesn't matter what your personal vision of success is. I've discovered there are some things you absolutely can't ignore when it comes to creating long-term success. At times I wasted countless hours trying to figure out a simple, easy way of doing business. But there is no one secret ingredient that guarantees success. In this chapter, we'll talk about how to achieve the best recipe for success by properly combining the skills and traits that make you unique.

If I had to look back on my business life and do it over again, I would have understood sooner that it was going to take time to find the right mix of ingredients for success. Even after collecting all the ingredients in the form of knowledge and skills, I discovered that each new business required a different mix. Not only did I need to learn new business skills, but I also needed to learn life skills—including patience—to help me survive and even thrive in challenging times.

Success Requires Patience

A personal life skill I still struggle with is patience. Many people feel the same way. When you want something, you want it now, and you want it without having to work for it. But there is no such thing as an overnight success. It takes time to build a business.

You need to gather the right mix of ingredients to blend together for the right amount of time, and you have to remain focused as you cook up your success. You can have the right ingredients, but if you stand in your own way by believing you are a bad cook, your personal limitations will get in the way of the success you desire. That is guaranteed!

Think about it: Business owners and entrepreneurs are confronted by their limitations every day. For example, learning the intricacies of sales and marketing may sound boring or intimidating. This is especially true when you have a lot to learn. Yet these skills are critically important to running any successful business. That's why I've devoted an entire chapter to them later in this book.

In this chapter you will discover that personal development is a big part of the success equation as well. So let's say you don't see the value in spending the time to work on personal development. Maybe you don't see how it will help you become more successful. Yet to improve and grow as a leader, personal development and improved life skills are vital to your success. It's all part of the secret recipe for success, and it helps make the formula work.

For example, a vision without commitment and determination is a wish. Commitment without a vision and determination is pointless. And determination without commitment and vision will not help you succeed either. It takes all three of these ingredients to mix up a good batch of success. Every successful person could share a slightly different recipe for their success, but overall they would agree that to succeed, you need the following mix:

THE RECIPE FOR SUCCESS

S—SELF-AWARE . . . of what success means to you

U—UNDERSTAND . . . that focused vision and goals are critical

C—CONFIDENCE . . . in moving away from limiting beliefs

C—COMMITMENT . . . to strategic action and calculated risks

E—EASY . . . with the right business skills and personal traits

S—SHAMELESS . . . by going for it and never giving up

S—STRONGER . . . with ongoing personal commitment to growth

Do you have all these ingredients in your own success recipe? Take a moment to journal some thoughts on each "ingredient," and try to pinpoint what you already have inside you and what you can start to cultivate. Then you will be ready to move on to building and amplifying your own set of success characteristics.

Seven Powerful Success-Building Characteristics

Successful people have many of the same characteristics in common. The following are seven highly successful characteristics that are critical to expand and build—in both business and life.

The Disrupter Mindset

Successful people passionately seek out opportunities for change or ways to disrupt their industry altogether. Learn how to break the rules to stand out in your industry.

Always look for the chance to profit from change and/or an innovative way to adjust how business is done so you can stand out and succeed. Don't get me wrong—you need to start with a useful idea. But when you think you have one, don't hold back. Take the core concept and turn up the disruption dial to the highest volume. For example, Sean and Thora Dowdell are the owners and founders of Club Tattoo, a chain of tattoo studios in Arizona and Nevada. They turned the tattoo business model on its head by avoiding the unapproachable atmosphere of typical tattoo parlors. Instead, Sean and Thora took a high-end, modern, customer service-focused approach to the studios and retail stores, which brought the tattoo business into the mainstream and built a multimillion-dollar business in the process.

A Vision for Opportunity

Successful people seek out opportunities everywhere. But finding good business opportunities isn't going to mean anything if you can't recognize them. Recognizing good opportunities takes talent, whether you are looking for something to really chase after or you already succeeded once in an area and wish to try again. You have to know what to look for and what to ask yourself, and you need to be able to envision the future of that opportunity.

Understanding what type of opportunity you're looking for and having a few goals in mind is crucial and will help determine which factors make it a good opportunity for you.

The first step is to remain on high alert to spot opportunities while remaining ruthlessly disciplined about limiting the number of projects you pursue. Go after a tightly controlled portfolio of opportunities in different stages of business development. Link your strategy with your choice of projects rather than diluting your efforts in many areas. Make quick decisions instead of over-analyzing new ideas, and execute a plan of action.

Shared Belief System

Successful people build a great support team. One characteristic of a strong supportive team is a shared belief in the same set of values. These same beliefs and values help create a bond so that the team works and supports one another. Shared values serve to connect team members at a core level, and this, in turn, serves to validate and strengthen their support for you as their leader. Their support continues to level up your success.

Begin to engage the energies of everyone inside and outside your organization in the pursuit of good opportunities. Successful people create and sustain powerful networks and business relationships rather than go it alone. You know how to best leverage the wisdom of experts and other resources to help achieve your goals. Business associates and joint venture partnerships can help move you miles ahead of your competitors.

Common Business Sense

Successful people have good common business sense and always looking for ways to continue educating themselves. Developing good business sense is about continually seeking to understand the ever-changing business environment. It is not a skill you can learn from a book. It's something you acquire through hands-on experience and trial and error, but it can also be fostered through the wisdom of others.

Brainstorming with seasoned business professionals gives you insight into how successful people with good business sense think and make decisions. Common business sense can be an amazing superpower that will help you achieve even more success!

Motivation to Learn

Successful people continue to learn with great enthusiasm and motivation, which are both key factors in learning. When you learn more about your business and successfully implement the strategies you discover, you become enthusiastic about learning even more.

Successful people become sponges to absorb anything that can help take their business to the next level. It's almost as if they can't get enough! Call them engaged, devoted, enthusiastic, or even obsessed—successful people believe in their mission so much that it's contagious to everyone around them, who marvel at their commitment and dedication. This energy can fuel you to remain focused on your mission and help you persist through difficulties.

Ability to Adapt

Successful people keep moving forward and adapt as needed. They have learned to change and reinvent their business often as the world and their industry change around them. If you fail to adapt, you will simply get left behind.

To keep growing, you must continuously think of ways to improve. Allow time in your busy schedule to learn new things and come up with new ideas. Successful people remain in constant motion by investing in learning because they are eager to pursue knowledge. They understand the world is always changing, so they need to adapt to avoid getting stuck in a rut. Successful people keep moving forward and reinvent themselves when required.

Observant Communicators

Successful people are observant communicators who pay close attention to how other people react. Communication is an activity, skill, and art that incorporates lessons across a wide spectrum of human knowledge.

One of the most likable characteristics of successful people is how observant they are. They give their full, undivided attention to others. Those who have mastered this are great communicators who go far in business. Successful people learn this skill by being more self-aware. Being observant requires practice to perfect.

These seven key characteristics and personal success traits keep you in motion in challenging times. Successful people learn to invest their time wisely in things that produce powerful results! These simple things move them forward every day, keeping them in constant pursuit of a creative purpose that inspires them. They often get three to ten times more accomplished in a day than the average person because they stay focused on what empowers them the most. They have chosen a life far beyond the norm, which means they think and act differently from the average person.

Successful People Think Differently

Education is not a key differentiator in success for the majority of us. Why is that? Because most people have a hard time being different. For success to come easily, it's going to require something different. Anything that keeps you stuck in the status quo guarantees mediocrity!

Successful people think differently and have different attitudes when it comes to business and life. They aren't afraid to be shameless and edgy when it's required. They are disciplined and self-motivated. Nothing will stop them. Refuse to take "no" for an answer, and knock down barriers to reach your goals if you have to.

Achieving an inspiring success breakthrough requires doing the opposite of what everyone else is doing. Never copy anyone else. You conquer more and are truer to yourself when you invest in being different!

Have an Edge

That kind of extreme differentiation means pushing the limits a little further than anyone else dares to. It means daring to have an edge.

It means understanding that the only limits that exist are the ones in your head.

What really stands in the way of your greatness isn't challenges, obstacles, or perceived limitations. What stands in your way is the misguided belief that what you want may be impossible. When you push the limits, you realize the impossible really isn't impossible after all. You grow when you gain the courage to push yourself beyond the norm, learn new skills, and gain traits and characteristics that add to your success mix. You become more shameless in your pursuit of success!

Don't Be a Know-It-All

Thinking you know it all is probably one of the worst self-limiting behaviors there is. It limits your ability to master new things, it limits your success, and it stalls your progress. It may be the excuse you use to stop educating yourself. Thinking you know it all limits your creativity and ability to explore new ideas. It keeps you from seeing the world outside your own limitations and personal judgments. When you catch yourself saying or thinking "I already know that," stop and think again!

Maximize Your People Skills

Much of your success in life hinges on your ability to understand people. Every decision in business is impacted by how well you relate to other people's communications, behaviors, and thoughts. Good people skills will improve your chances for success and help you win in business and in life.

The ability to work well with people tops the list for the most common business skills and habits of highly successful people. In fact, research conducted by Harvard University, the Carnegie Foundation, and Standard Research Center has shown that 85 percent of job success comes from having well-developed soft and people skills, and only 15 percent of job success comes from technical skills and knowledge (hard skills). Yet nowhere in the formal education system, from kindergarten through college, are people skills taught.

That leaves you having to learn people skills on the job, through networking and interacting with others every day. In the next section, I'll walk you through ten easy ways you can level up your people skills.

Ten Simple Ways to Improve Your People Skills

No matter what new technologies and systems you put in place to grow your business, how to work with people will always matter most. To develop natural charm and innate people skills requires effort along with trial and error. Here are ten simple ways to help improve your natural charm and create real connections to build more powerful people skills.

1. Talk to Others About What They Want to Hear

People often hear only what they want or need. The things potential customers want to hear most are how you serve their goals, interests, ideas, experiences, and aspirations. Talk about that, and you will get and hold their attention without difficulty.

2. Take a Training Course

Invest in learning how to communicate more effectively. This will pay off in every aspect of your business and personal life. The highest-paid and most powerful people on the planet are all master communicators that have learned how to take control of even the most challenging situations, understand the art of persuasion, and know how to recognize and use persuasive strategies. Good communication leads to success!

3. Show Appreciation

Make it a habit to thank others for everything they do to support you. A simple "thank you" makes others feel appreciated. You benefit in return by having good feelings about making others feel good. And you also benefit by making others think better of you, making them want to do more good things for you in return. The more you genuinely show others you care, the easier it will be to make a good impression on them.

4. Give Genuine, Sincere Compliments

When you compliment someone about a trait, skill, accomplishment, or possession, it gives them feelings of recognition and value. The more you pay close attention to customers, the more important they feel. When you pay compliments often, even on small things, it helps you build rapport.

5. Act Honorably and Treat Others with Respect

Always do the right thing, even when no one is watching. That's how you build a positive business reputation. Reputation is not purchased; it is earned. We've all heard this: "Nobody cares how much you know until they know how much you care." This is the Golden Rule in business that should govern your attitudes, thoughts, words, and actions.

6. Identify Personal Core Values

Clarifying your core values highlights what you stand for. Your core values also represent your uniqueness and personal style. They guide your behavior and provide you with a personal code of conduct. When you honor your core values consistently, you experience fulfillment in every part of life. And when you don't, you become incongruent in your business practices.

For example, if one of your core values is to offer high-quality customer service, yet your employees don't show customers the respect they deserve, that's a problem because you're working outside your core business values. To turn it around, you must empower your team to match every area of your core values, including valuing customers.

7. Commit to Good Business Ethics

Practicing good business ethics should go without saying. So why are there still so many unethical businesspeople out there? Ethics are your moral judgment about what is right and what is wrong. Good ethics simply make good business sense!

Success comes easily when you act with honesty and integrity at all times. Good ethics require dealing honestly in your business, backing up your products and services, and treating everyone fairly. A lack of business ethics endangers your future success and jeopardizes your reputation. If you believe that, like karma, what goes around comes around, always practice good ethics.

8. Remain True to Your Authentic Self

Remaining true to your beliefs helps you sincerely connect to others. Pretending to be something you're not makes doing business hard. You can't manipulate your personality to seek approval or avoid disapproval.

Authenticity is not defined by your title, position, or role. It is all about being true to your heart and your destiny. This requires you to trust yourself, embrace your uniqueness, share your gifts, and learn to be present in the moment.

For example, one of the greatest compliments I get from audience members after giving a speech is, "You are so real and authentic. I felt like you were speaking directly to me." Hearing this always warms my heart. It's my goal to always be in the moment, make a personal connection (no matter how large the audience is), and share my knowledge with the audience. It's about connecting your head and heart to make an impact.

9. Build Confidence to Make Stronger Connections

Being confident earns you the respect of others. Confidence shows in many ways, including your mannerisms, appearance, and the way you talk, walk, and listen to people. To become more confident, you must respect and accept yourself as you are right now. You are unique in your own way. Accepting yourself and your flaws without any inner conflict helps build confidence.

Take responsibility for your success by having confidence, which is independent of all external factors, especially those things beyond your control. Confident people talk assertively, strike an assured pose, and use a certain tone of voice. Confidence allows you to be tough in business, but tough doesn't mean you can't still be friendly and approachable. Having true confidence is about being daringly honest and truthful at all times.

10. Tackle Problems with a Positive Mental Attitude

Positive thinking allows you to try to solve problems through constructive action. A positive mental attitude lets you build strengths and overcome weaknesses. It helps you realize you're born for greatness because within you is the power to make any dream a reality.

Create More Positive Vibrations

Staying positive allows you to pay attention to all the goodness surrounding you, keep your mind off what you don't want, and focus on what you do want. Negative people focus mainly on what they don't want by constantly complaining about how the world is unfair. And who wants to be around a negative person who drains your energy? Not anyone I know!

So start creating more positive vibrations to improve your positivity. Think of it like this: What you focus on, you create more of. Having a positive attitude helps generate a powerful magnetism to attract more success into your life.

Nothing good ever comes out of knee-jerk reactions or negative, stressed-out remarks. They only cause panic. It takes time for the dust to settle and conditions to stabilize when things go wrong. Business needs this reaction time as well. When you maintain a positive, upbeat attitude and send those vibrations out into the world, you can focus on a better possible outcome.

True Success Begins by Giving Back

Successful people care about supporting others, rather than manipulating them and keeping everything to themselves. The spirit of giving back is the very essence of a successful life.

Giving doesn't have a planned return on investment. By definition, it's an investment without an expected return. You set yourself up for disappointment when you pretend to give selflessly, secretly expecting the recipient to give you something back in return. That's not how it works!

Giving requires a positive mindset that focuses on others first. It means you see your efforts in the context of something bigger and greater. It can take some people a lifetime of striving for success before they can consider giving back. It is often after achieving success that people consider giving back. But what would happen if, instead of waiting until success arrives at your doorstep, you began to give back now?

Giving is contrary to the way most people live in this competitive, dog-eat-dog world. For the most part, people concern themselves with making their star shine brightly while ignoring those around them.

But what if success requires a different approach? You can get ahead by changing your view from taking to giving. You'll find that you receive more in return.

Monetary and professional success is the very foundation of a successful life. Yet true success begins when you decide to give back

Look for every opportunity to think and act differently. Master the ability to view success in a unique way. Promote your own personal style, but do it in a way to give back to others in return.

to others. It sometimes takes a startling reminder to appreciate how much you have to give. Success means celebrating those around you and cheering others on so you can all become your very best selves. For example, I love sharing my own success with others. Every time I have a big win, I try to find a way to share that win with a business associate or client so that they can experience a win too. I do this by thinking of a way to share a referral for business or by putting them into the loop for the same type of opportunity. And what I've discovered is that the more I share more success, the more success comes to me in return. There's plenty to go around—so why not share.

Shameless, No-Nonsense Action Steps and Affirmation

Success Is Easy Affirmation (say it, believe it, and own it): "Success comes easy to me because I have the right mix of business skills and personal traits."

1. *Develop new success-building skills and traits to create your own recipe for success.* Achieving success is just like following a recipe. When you put in the right ingredients, it results in delicious rewards. But running a successful business requires a mix of the right skills and personal traits. You can have the right mix of ingredients, but if you stand in your own way by believing you are a "bad cook," your personal limitations will block the success you desire. That is guaranteed!

2. *Push the limits.* When you push your limits, you may realize the impossible really isn't impossible after all. Differentiating yourself from others means pushing the limits a little further than anyone else dares to. It means daring to have an edge. It means understanding that the only limits that exist are the ones in your head.

3. *Develop good people skills.* Much of your success hinges on your ability to understand, relate to, and connect with others effectively. The ability to work well with people tops the list for the most common business skills and habits of

highly-successful people. Studies show that as much as 85 percent of success in life depends on our people skills and the ability to get others to like us. Yet nowhere in the formal education system, from kindergarten through college, are people skills taught. You'll need to learn this on your own.

4. *Support others by finding ways to give back.* Monetary and professional success is the very foundation of a successful life. Yet true success begins when you decide to give back to others. Giving requires a positive mindset that focuses on others first. It means you see the results of your discipline and success in the context of something bigger and greater.

5. *Take responsibility for your success by having confidence!* Being confident is respected by others. Confidence is shown in many ways, including our mannerisms, appearance, and the way you talk, walk, and listen to people. To become more confident, you must respect and accept yourself as you are right now. You are unique in your own way. Accepting ourselves and our flaws, without any inner conflict, helps build confidence.

SUCCESS IS EASY . . .
with a Strong Marketing Foundation

Position yourself for success by developing a strong marketing foundation from the start. This foundation includes a good marketing plan and unique brand positioning that best fits the vision and target market for your business.

One of the most important aspects of a good marketing foundation is a vision for future growth. When a house is built, the strength of its foundation is key to building something that will last for years. The foundation of a house is the anchor that supports the entire structure, holding it strong and steady despite changes and challenges from outside forces.

The same is true for your business, which must have a strong foundation to create an environment in which it can grow, expand, and prosper.

In this chapter, you will see the importance of building a brand foundation and a marketing platform. You will learn why it's critical to get crystal clear about the foundation of your business first. When you have nailed down the marketing and brand foundation, the right doors of opportunity will open for you.

Marketing Is Like Fishing

I like to think of marketing like fishing. When you go fishing, you find out where the fish are and then go there to catch some. First, you have to get the proper bait, put it on the hook, throw out the line, and reel it back in to change the bait every so often. Then you repeat the process and wait. If you try long enough and keep testing the bait, you will catch some fish.

The same is true for marketing. When you are doing it well, you see results and hook some prospects! It might take some time before the process works to catch a prospect. You might even need to switch the bait by trying new marketing strategies. But if you keep changing it up and keep at it long enough, you will get customers!

Instead of worms, you use words to bait your prospects. If your words don't work, a lot of (fish) or customers get away. If your prospects don't take the bait because they don't understand the message (the value of what you're all about), they won't bite the hook.

When you believe there are potential clients out there looking for you, the words in your marketing message must carry energy to bite into. Translating marketing words into a language almost anyone can understand makes it easy for people to take the bait and buy from you!

Brand Message Consistency

A clearly defined brand is the foundation for good business. It articulates the authenticity, benefits, and characteristics of a business.

Your brand also showcases the value and benefits of doing business with you and differentiates your business from your competitors. The purpose of a brand foundation is to ensure consistency in how your brand is communicated. Ultimately, your brand is what allows you to build recognition, trust, and loyalty.

Don't confuse personal identity with business brand. A well-designed logo or attractive website is just one aspect of a brand. Brand is everything from how you communicate internally to how the business is perceived externally. It's critical to leverage a brand to its fullest potential and use it with 100 percent consistency across the board.

Business and Brand Strategy Go Hand in Hand

Your business brand sets the tone and direction for where your business is headed. If you are reinventing or redesigning the brand identity, reworking the brand is the first step in redesigning your overall marketing strategy.

Your brand allows others to understand what your business is all about and connect with, understand, and recognize you as the best in your industry. It's the first step to building trusting relationships with prospects.

Effective branding moves your business in the right direction, but the wrong brand image can move the business miles away from the target market. You must have a way to stand out to your ideal target client—especially in today's noisy marketplace—if you want to catch a boatload of fish.

People want to invest in businesses because of the know, like, and trust factors. A great brand will give you that edge. When done effectively, your brand connects to your overall business strategy and

Standing out means moving away from "The Sea of Sameness" and owning what you do!

goals. Your brand is everything that represents you and what your business is all about. It must have a unique voice.

Develop a Solid Brand Promise

Creating a brand promise allows a company to grow wisely. Once a brand is developed, the first step toward success is to create an ongoing promise and commitment to customers. Make sure the brand promise is simple and clear enough to be understood, remembered, and embraced by the right prospects.

There are two ways in which customers form an impression about your brand. There is the "perceptual experience," which comes from all the ways your message is heard. It's about your brand's voice: advertising, word-of-mouth, website, social media, etc. Then there is the "actual experience," which comes from the buying process and is based on the quality of service, product, delivery, price, and investment.

If a customer's perceptual experience is greater than the actual experience, they will reject the business brand. If, on the other hand, the actual experience exceeds expectations, they will continue to support the brand and the organization.

The second step in creating a brand promise requires a shared mission that is shaped and delivered by everyone in the organization. Many organizations start off with a simple idea, but over time, things tend to get added on to the original offer, either by the owner or the team. And while these small things don't really seem to matter at the time, each one weakens the brand and business foundation.

The third step is to develop the brand from the inside out by investing in ongoing training and education. Emphasis on teamwork is crucial to helping every member of the team understand their role as brand champions.

See Your Marketing Foundation from a Clearer Viewpoint

It's hard to have a vision beyond the current focus on your business. You are too close to your business to see why you can't grow, get more customers, or create more sales. In reality, you may be stuck or just unable to figure out how to grow beyond your current marketing foundation. This may be due to a block in your marketing plan or overall business growth strategy.

Whether you're starting, reinventing, or expanding your business, get crystal clear about the foundation first! When you have firmly established the marketing and brand foundation, the doors will open to the right target market.

In working with a diverse set of consulting clients, I've discovered they have one thing in common: They are all too close to their business to see the blocks that are stopping them from growing.

My clients have diverse business backgrounds. Some are new business owners with startup companies who need to build a foundation from the ground up. These startups have the biggest challenge when it comes to their foundation, as they often don't understand their ideal target market and don't know how to clearly articulate the uniqueness of their business.

Already-successful clients often need to implement new marketing strategies and learn new skills to help take their sales and income to the next level. Again, they are too close to their business to see the problem clearly.

For example, while working with franchises, I can see that their foundation can become faulty once a franchisee stops showing loyalty to the brand and the overall marketing strategies developed by the organization. I love the fact that franchises offer new business owners and entrepreneurs a proven business model with an established brand and a strong foundation already in place. This business model creates an opportunity to capitalize on a built-in operating system between the franchisor and the franchisee, as well as within the community of franchises. Yet with multiple locations and a variety of franchise owners, it's often challenging to keep their foundation intact.

Franchise relationships offer a unique chance to work in tandem with other business owners, but this requires effective communication on both sides to ensure success. The franchisor doesn't always know how to best empower franchisees to deliver the same high-quality results that were built into their foundation from the start. That's where I come in, working to help keep the foundation strong for both corporate leadership and the franchise business owners.

Seven Insights to Help Build a Strong Marketing Foundation

No matter the level of your business, it's important to have a clear picture of how your marketing foundation is or is not leading toward growth. Let's do that now. Take a few moments to journal some answers to the questions below. Respond to each of the following questions with specific details to help you gain more clarity. Don't get too general or grandiose with your answers. The goal is to be realistic and honest. Ask yourself:

1. What truly sets your business, services, and products apart from your competitors?
2. What unique customer service do you provide that your competitors don't?
3. How do you best describe your ideal target market?
4. If you could wave a magic wand and move your business into the future, what would that look like?
5. What are some personal challenges holding you back from growing your business to the next level?
6. What areas of marketing need more focus to grow your business?
7. Will your current business foundation support the growth you wish to achieve in the future?

After evaluating your answers, you will begin to gain clarity on the direction you should be taking your brand and marketing foundation.

Build an Effective Marketing Strategy

One of the most important aspects of growing a business is the marketing strategy. With an effective marketing strategy in place, it's easy to take on many potential growth opportunities. Good marketing allows you to find out who your actual customers are, as opposed to who you think they are. It also tells you how to acquire more customers and where to spend your marketing dollars.

Business owners and entrepreneurs who do not create a marketing strategy are destined to either fail or struggle indefinitely. However, just creating a strategy does not guarantee success.

To develop a proven marketing strategy, you must first understand your target market and know how to reach them. When you know this, good marketing will never cost you anything because it always pays off. Good marketing also communicates your value. In this competitive business world, marketing is more about effective communication than anything else. One way you do that is by putting the customer first.

Taking care of your customers is one of the smartest and lowest-cost marketing strategies you can implement. When you focus on giving value to customers, your company will grow naturally. Putting customers first also helps distinguish you from the competition. When you show you care, it is reflected in your services, products, and overall business.

A passion for caring is the foundation for success. If you don't have passion at the outset, you'll never have it in the long run. Simply stated, people can tell when a company doesn't care about its customers, and eventually, your customers will stop caring, too.

> Once you implement your brand marketing strategy, be true to it in everything you do.

Shameless, No-Nonsense Action Steps and Affirmation

Success Is Easy Affirmation (say it, believe it, and own it): "Success comes easy to me because I've built a strong marketing foundation for my business."

1. *Develop a clearly defined brand that articulates the authenticity, benefits, and characteristics of your business.* This allows

you to stand out from your competition and focus on your ideal target market. The business brand sets the tone and direction for where your business is headed. Your brand helps others understand what your business is all about. A brand allows others to connect, understand, and recognize why you are the best at something. Effective branding moves your business in the right direction.

2. *Develop a solid brand promise and commitment to your customers.* Make sure the brand promise is simple and clear enough to be understood, remembered, and embraced by the target prospects. Customers form an impression about your brand in two ways. There is the "perceptual experience," which comes from all the ways your message is heard: advertising, word-of-mouth, website, social media, etc. Then there is the "actual experience," which comes from the buying process and is based on the quality of your service, product, delivery, price, investment, etc. Every part of your brand should make a connection as your overall brand promise.

3. *Establish a clear direction for where the business is heading so you can adjust and reinforce your marketing foundation.* Whether you're starting a new business or reinventing or expanding an existing one, get crystal clear about the foundation first! When you have a firmly established marketing and brand foundation, doors will open for you and the right target market will find you.

4. *Realize that good marketing never costs anything because it always pays off.* Good marketing helps to clearly communicate your value and attract new prospects with ease. In this competitive business world, good marketing is more about effective communication than anything else.

5. *Always put customers first.* Taking care of your customers is one of the smartest and lowest-cost marketing strategies you can implement. A passion for caring is the foundation for your success.

proven success principles to win in business

SUCCESS IS EASY . . .
with Vision
and Direction

S uccess begins with a good idea and a clear vision, which can guide you toward the short-term and long-term results you desire. To paraphrase the old adage: You must see it before you can achieve it.

A strong mental picture can propel you toward success even when there is no logical basis for it. When you see a vision clearly in your mind, a creative "success mechanism" takes over. This is when your inner guide begins to activate success effortlessly using and directing the subconscious mind to achieve what you desire. When you provide a clear, defined vision, your mind subconsciously helps guide you toward your goals.

This natural instinct was best described by Maxwell Maltz, author of the book *Psycho-Cybernetics*. He described the same energy in relation to how plants grow or squirrels gather nuts for winter; the same automatic "success mechanism" will naturally direct you, too. In fact, it often does a much better job than you can with a conscious effort.

In this chapter, you will discover how to become a powerful visionary who can take an idea or thought and craft it into your own vision for success. You will then learn how to take complete ownership of your vision and take specific action steps to achieve what you want.

Seeing Is Believing

To begin, you must be able to see your goal before you can believe in it, whatever "it" may be. When you can see where you are going, you begin to attract the circumstances and the people you need to accomplish that goal. You have the power to mentally create a new life for yourself by visualizing it.

Visualization is a technique for creating a mental image of a future event. When visualizing a desired outcome, you begin to see the possibility of achieving it. Through visualization, you catch a glimpse of your preferred future, which motivates and inspires you to pursue your goals.

Do not confuse visualization with the "think it and you will be it" advice touted by many self-help gurus. It is not a gimmick, and it does not mean you can sit still and hope for success. Rather, visualization is a well-developed method of performance improvement supported by substantial scientific evidence and used by nearly all successful people.

The first question I ask anyone who talks with me about growing their business is "Where do you see yourself and your business a year from now?" Building a highly successful business comes down to first gaining clarity about exactly what you want. This helps you create a clear path that moves you in the right direction from the beginning, and it starts by seeing yourself already achieving your goal.

Visualization Helps Set Intention

I don't believe in "woo-woo" concepts or self-development fluff. Although I've read dozens of self-help books and attended numerous personal-development seminars, I still want proof these concepts work in real life. I once attended a personal-development workshop in Sedona, Arizona, that was hosted by one of my clients, Dr. Dolores Fazzino, founder of Spiritual Wellness for Life. At one point during a visualization exercise, she asked us to draw an image on a piece of paper that looked and felt like something we wanted to manifest into our lives.

As I sat there and pondered what I wanted to manifest, thoughts of a new home came to mind. I started to build that house in my mind. I drew a circle in the middle of the page and added lines coming out from it. It looked like a sun with rays shooting out from the center. Inside the circle, I wrote, "I love my new home." On the lines, I wrote everything I saw and felt in and around the home, including a large kitchen, beautiful office, courtyard, large patio full of flowering plants, a conference room where I could work with my clients, a spacious guesthouse, and more.

My husband and I had talked about building a house someday that fit both our business and our lifestyle, but we had no concrete plans of when or where. Yet in a little more than a year after I drew this picture, we were living in the dream home I had envisioned. It had

Vision paints the picture that
fuels the passion to take action.
Action is the fire that allows you
to pursue your vision aggressively.

everything I had seen and felt in my vision. When I set the intention in my subconscious, it led me to discover the resources I needed to make it happen.

This type of visual manifestation has showed up many times in my life. At times it has almost felt magical. The power of visualization will work for anyone who is open to it—including you. You just have to find a method that works for you.

BIG VISIONARIES CREATE MASSIVE SUCCESS

Honoring your vision is not a new concept. Many people use it to their benefit, including successful celebrities. Let's look at a few examples.

In the mid-1980s, Jim Carrey was an unknown actor struggling to get by. To stay motivated, he decided to write himself a check for $10 million for "acting services rendered." He postdated the check for Thanksgiving 1995 and carried it in his wallet for daily inspiration. Just before the check's deadline, he learned he would be given $10 million for his role in the movie *Dumb and Dumber*. Carrey credits this power of visualization for his amazing success. He would even park up on Mulholland Drive and visualize his future success to help keep himself motivated.

Lindsey Vonn is one of the most successful female skiers in history, and she states it was her mental practice that gave her an advantage. She would visualize the ski course up to a hundred times in her mind before coming out of the gate. She pictured every turn and felt every movement. This visualization technique helped her win an Olympic gold medal and two World Championship gold medals, as well as four overall World Cup championships.

As a young athlete, Arnold Schwarzenegger swore by the power of visualization to reach his bodybuilding goals. He had a fixed idea of what he wanted his ideal body to look like. The more he focused on the image, the more he saw it as real and possible. He began living as if that picture were already true, leading to five Mr. Universe and seven Mr. Olympia titles. As he transitioned to an acting and later a political career, he used the same mental visualization techniques to help achieve success.

Focus on the Big Picture

To begin your own visualization process, focus first on the big picture—be acutely aware of your overall goal and how it fits into your world. When you work on improving your own awareness, you also develop more powerful visualization skills. Every decision you make and every action you take is based on your level of awareness. When your awareness increases, your visualization also improves.

Good visualizers become "big-picture thinkers." This is a process that expands not only what you see but also what you are able to achieve. Big-picture thinkers are never satisfied with the status quo. They want to discover new ways of seeing things outside the ordinary.

For example, much of Albert Einstein's celebrated success came from his imagination, which worked in very nonscientific ways. His accomplishments stand as testaments to the ability to rise above and beyond existing knowledge, education, experience, or skill through the power of visualization.

Big-picture thinkers recognize that they don't know everything and frequently ask others for help. They ask questions to enlarge their understanding and learn to see the bigger picture in every opportunity because it expands their experiences and their world. As a result, they accomplish more than narrow-minded people with limited vision.

Big-picture thinking allows you to experience more success. When you keep the whole picture in mind, you stay on target—even with your daily achievements.

Set Your Intention

Next, set your sights on what you want, also known as setting your intention. To set your intention, write it out in great detail, but stay focused on the big picture and the final outcome. Describe not only the achievement itself, but also how you will feel once you achieve it. This is much more than just writing out your goals. Take time to visualize the picture as if you have already achieved your goal. The more senses and perspectives your vision contains, the more powerful the big picture will become.

To get started, find a quiet place away from your home and office and sit alone. Write and listen to your inner promptings. Trust the flow. Let intuition guide the process from one thought to another.

Consider these questions: Where do you want to be in life and business six months from now? One year from now? Three years from now?

For example, think about how much money you want to make in the coming year, what type of clients you want to work with, where you want to work, how much you want to travel, etc.

Also keep in mind that your ambitions are often based on what you feel you are worthy of at the time. You should stretch the possibilities because the ideas you write down are very likely to become reality.

To move toward setting higher and bigger goals, clarify which things bring you the most joy, fulfillment, and feelings of success. This is where you will gain the most visual insight.

Pay close attention to the people who are placed in front of you for support. As you do, support and information will begin to appear out of nowhere. This is no accident—these are your inner promptings working for you.

Listen to Your Inner Promptings

Visualization also gives you the courage to listen to your inner promptings for a hint of the kind of success you truly desire. Start by thinking about where you want to go and talk to yourself about it every day. Look back at this exercise a year from now, and you'll be amazed at how far you've come.

Visualization and imagination are the most powerful tools you can use to go from where you are to where you want to be.

I see this happen with my clients all the time. I often ask, "Who are you? What happened to that person I met a year ago?" It's astonishing to see how fast visualization and direction can guide people to change both professionally and personally when they are open to it.

If you don't know what your inner promptings are telling you, it's difficult to manage your actions because you haven't identified or decided on any yet. Most people have dozens of things to do to make progress on many fronts, but they don't take action because their ultimate direction is unclear.

Even with a clear vision and all the proper knowledge in place, success is often achieved with a shameless "fake it until you make it" approach. You often need to trust your inner promptings to guide success before you figure out all the details or understand the "how."

The "How" Is None of Your Business

There is a vast amount of information available to support how your vision will play out. For now, you don't need to worry about the "how." Most people try to figure out the details and make comments that bring the creative visualization process to a halt, such as:

- "I don't know where the money's coming from."
- "I don't know what it takes to make this happen."
- "I don't have enough experience to pull this off."

Trying to figure out things like this will cloud your vision. It will either slow you down or stop you from achieving your vision altogether. You don't have to get all the facts laid out before taking action. Success doesn't work that way.

For now, the "how" is none of your business. Simply set the intention and allow your inner promptings to guide your actions. Don't wait to put your ideas into motion. Resources and results will begin to show up when you pay attention and take action.

Here is a list of questions to help you visualize and clarify your ideas and action steps:

- What has worked so far to help you grow both personally and professionally? Why has it worked?
- What do you need to do to expand on that knowledge and wisdom going forward in the direction of your goals?
- What overall vision inspires and motivates you to do and be more?
- What specific vision do you wish to create for your business and income within one year?

- What are you 100 percent committed to achieving?
- What intention have you set into action to help you create something you wanted in the past?
- What information can you learn that will direct you more effectively?
- If failure is not an option, what daily action do you take to create a never-quit attitude?

The process of writing out your intentions in great detail will help you gain clarity and focus specifically on the success-driven goals you desire. As you take action, review your intentions to make sure you are on the right path. They may need slight adjustments, shifts, or changes to redirect you along the way.

Put Your Big Vision into Action

Vision alone is certainly not enough to make things magically happen. Success is achieved by much more than wishful thinking. You must move from the visualization process to action to achieve your goals. Without a plan, most business owners and entrepreneurs will get overwhelmed and frustrated. Some will simply give up.

A strong vision will help deepen your awareness. Awareness directs action, which leads to opportunity. You'll know you're on the right path when your hard work becomes easy. Below are three steps to putting your big vision into action:

1. *Work backwards.* It may be easier to work backwards than to start from where you are now. This will help you see the end result more clearly. It's less daunting and creates a no-nonsense check-in on how realistic your vision actually is.
2. *Get the timing and focus right.* You may need more or less time to achieve your vision. Let's say your vision is a far stretch from where you are right now. For example, it's not likely to imagine you can go from making $50,000 a year to $1 million a year with the same knowledge, skills, and opportunities. That may be an exciting vision, but you also need to be realistic. Give yourself enough time to achieve your goals.

You also don't want your vision to be too limited. Even if your business is small, that doesn't mean your vision needs to be. To raise the level of your vision, yet still be realistic, you can set yourself more challenging goals. When you learn to become a powerful visionary with clear and focused direction, your perception will become your reality!

3. *Nurture your vision.* The vision can fade without continual nurturing. You must remain excited, committed, and motivated to achieve it at all times. To envision your future success, it's vital to expand what you see for yourself far beyond where you are now.

Affirmations and Emotion Add Motivation to Your Vision

Putting your vision into action also involves some positive self-talk in the form of affirmations.

Affirmations "affirm" what you believe to be true about yourself and your level of success.

Affirmations are intentional statements that when spoken aloud will guide you. They play a big role in supporting your visions and goals (that's why I have included one at the end of each chapter). The words you speak about yourself have guided you to where you are right now. Intentional statements either lead you to success or keep you from success.

Another way to increase the power of visualization is by adding feelings or emotions to what you see. Once you feel the emotions of your accomplishments, even before you have achieved them, those emotions will help motivate and direct you toward your vision.

Affirmation + Visualization + Emotion = Success!

GOING FOR IT!

By combining the power of affirmation, visualization, and emotion, I was able to launch my professional speaking business. At the time, I didn't have good speaking skills or understand the "how," but that didn't stop me.

It started with a simple idea and the passion to support business owners. In a conversation with one of my sales reps at a Las Vegas trade show, while I was purchasing merchandise for my retail stores, I said, "Why hold this huge trade show without providing educational seminars to support the success of the attendees? In fact, I could teach a class like that!"

He replied, "You would be great at that. You've had so much success growing your businesses, you could help a lot of people. I know the manager of the show. I'll introduce you to him."

This short exchange launched my speaking business. I didn't know a thing about becoming a professional speaker or filling a seminar room, but I promised the trade show manager I would pack the seminar to standing-room only. I needed to prove that his investment in my presentation would pay off and the seminars would benefit his show and the attendees.

Now how was I going to pull it off? I had the vision and the motivation; now I needed to look for resources.

Next I asked the trade show manager to promote the seminar on the front page of the event newspaper and the direct-mail postcards. I also asked him to host the seminar on the third day of the trade show so I would have more time to fill the seats. I worked the trade show shamelessly, asking my sales reps to pass out fliers promoting the seminar. I also rode the shuttle bus back and forth from the hotel to the event, asking people, "What are you doing tomorrow morning? Attend my success seminar!" This got attendees' attention and helped fill more seats.

Shameless? Yes!

Successful? Also yes!

By the day of the seminar I had pulled off what seemed impossible: a morning seminar in Las Vegas where people go out and play all night, making morning seminars less than appealing.

This first successful seminar launched my professional speaking career 25 years ago.

If you allow limiting emotions such as doubt to get in the way, it will slow your progress. For example, one of my core values in business is to make it challenging and fun. With my true entrepreneurial spirit, I get bored if I'm not challenged and enjoying my work. Therefore, my motto is, "If it's not fun, I'm not going to do it anymore!" I pay very close attention when these feelings arise. When they do, I know it's time to refocus and create some exciting, fun, and challenging visions to chase.

Set an Easy Affirmation for What's Possible

The adjective "easy" can apply to almost anything in life. Using this word in my affirmations has had a profound effect on my results. Like most people, I like doing things that are easy rather than things that are hard. Using the word "easy" helps trigger my mind to move projects and outcomes along faster. It creates a positive expectation of a successful outcome in a short amount of time.

Stating goals in a positive, present-tense statement keeps it clear in your mind. Use positive self-talk every day and reward even small achievements. Build a mental picture of success and envision living the dream already.

Increase Your Success Rate

Affirmations are a great way to focus inward, improve your chances of success, and enhance your self-esteem. Using affirmations can help you prioritize what is important to you and set you on the road to opportunity. Below are some examples of positive affirmations that will raise your success rate:

- I am worthy of success in every area of my life.
- I'm attracting everything I need to become more successful.
- I pursue and achieve my goals with drive and determination.
- I climb over any obstacle that gets in the way of my success.
- I believe in myself and my abilities to succeed beyond my wildest dreams.
- Opportunity, success, and money flow to me freely and easily.

- I create incredible opportunities that show up effortlessly in my life and my business.
- I am clear and focused, which allows me to level up my success.

Now that you have selected your positive affirmations, start putting them to work for you. Your affirmation has the ability to work for you because it programs your mind into believing what it's been told is true. This is because the mind doesn't know the difference between what is real or fantasy. For example, when you watch a movie you can become completely engaged in what's going on which may cause you to react in laugher or tears. You are not personally connected to the actors in the movie, but your mind is making the connection feel real in that moment. The same is true for how you can "shift" your mind's belief around an affirmation.

You can expect different levels of success depending on how committed you are to your affirmations. But when you add visualization to your positive affirmation, you can expect to increase your success rate even more.

Visualization will actually help you achieve your goals when you use it to envision the outcome you wish to reach. According to research using brain imagery, visualization works because neurons in our brains, interpret imagery as equivalent to a real-life action. Therefore, when you visualize an action, your brain generates an impulse that creates action towards hat you've imagined.

Now fire up your imagination to envision your best self and ideal business success. Get creative and have fun with it! Let go of the need to know everything from the start. Give up your worries and your need for perfectionism. There is no such thing as perfection, so don't even try. Instead, envision being the best possible you that you can be. Human. Imperfect. Amazing!

Shameless, No-Nonsense Action Steps and Affirmation

Success Is Easy Affirmation (say it, believe it, and own it): "Success comes easy to me because I commit to positive affirmations and use visualization to envision a successful outcome to my goals."

1. *Clearly envision where you see yourself and your business a year from now.* Visualization helps set your intention for success. A strong mental picture can pull you toward success even when there is no logical argument for it. When you see a vision clearly in your mind, your creative "success mechanism" takes over, using and directing your subconscious mind to provide what you desire. When your mind has a clear, defined vision, it gives you subconscious guidance that directs you toward your goals.

2. *Focus on the big picture.* Every decision you make and every action you take is based on a level of awareness. Once your awareness increases, your visualization also improves. Where do you see yourself and your business a year from now? Knowing this is the key to gaining clarity and getting exactly what you want. It allows you to create a clear path to move you in the right direction from the beginning and provides a vision to see yourself already achieving the goal.

3. *Set your intention on the big picture.* Write it out in great detail, focusing on the final outcome. Describe not only the achievement itself, but also how you will feel once you achieve it. The more senses and perspectives your vision contains, the more powerful your big picture will become.

4. *Become a powerful visionary.* When you learn how to create a clear and focused direction, perception becomes your reality. Visualization will give you the courage to listen to your inner promptings to figure out what kind of success you truly desire. Start by knowing where you want to go and talk to yourself about it every day. When you look back a year from now, you'll be amazed at how far you've come. Visualization and imagination are the most powerful tools you can use to get from where you are right now to where you want to be.

5. *Create intentional affirmations to motivate your vision.* Spoken and written affirmations play a big role in supporting your vision and your goals. Affirmations are a great way to focus inward and improve your chances for success. Speaking

affirmations can help you prioritize what is important to you and set you on the road to opportunity. Choose positive affirmations and repeat them daily to level up your success opportunities.

SUCCESS IS EASY . . .
with Focus on Business Basics

It shocks me to see how many business owners and entrepreneurs continue to get in their own way by focusing on the wrong things in business. There is no reason to make success hard when it is easy. Focusing on failure or success requires equal amounts of energy. You have incredible potential for greatness. You just need to learn how to tap into it.

Don't try focusing on what you don't know at first, or it will get you frustrated and stuck. Focus instead on what you CAN do and keep going to gain momentum.

This means you should focus on the easy parts first. Then you can come back to the more difficult aspects of building your business. Hopefully by then you'll have built up enough momentum that it won't break your productive focus.

In this chapter, you will read about the importance of remaining focused on the basic business skills (especially soft skills) that drive you to success with ease. Those basic skills, from everyday motivation and multitasking to broad project-development goals and decision making, are what truly set you up for success. When you keep your attention on the action steps that get you closer to fulfilling your dreams, you will continue to move toward success. Focus often pays off more than brilliance when it comes to running a successful business because it allows you to remain clear, consistent, and committed to your goals.

Focus on What Works for Easy Success

Many business owners believe they will succeed, but they lack the basic business skills and common business sense to back up that belief. Therefore, they waste a lot of time focusing on expensive details. Instead, focus on the things that will make your success easier!

Begin with the basic business skills and principles that are proven to work. I mentor business owners and support them in building or reinventing their businesses. Part of this process is to develop or re-create their branding. Occasionally, I get a client who gets stuck wasting time and energy on details such as perfecting the color or the font on the logo when he should be focusing on income-generating

What you focus on the most
will either move you forward
or hold you back.

areas of the business that generate profits. People like this make it hard, instead of making it easy by trusting the process.

Small details such as this are important, but they require a limited amount of time and focus. Obsessing over perfection or the wrong details is not cost-effective. You must learn how to prioritize. Know how much time to spend on each aspect of your business, and don't waste time on less important tasks.

Business is a matter of using your practical experience, good common sense, and your ability to foresee and prepare for the future. Here's the good news: You can learn anything you need to know about business to become as successful as you want to be.

The basic business skills you need to learn for success include marketing, sales, service, systems, finance, team building, and how to effectively manage growth. By mastering these business basics, you'll gain the knowledge you need to make money, which will allow you to invest in the support systems you need to grow the business. But you must remain focused on the right things and move in the right direction, or you'll get derailed.

Lack of direction causes many businesses to fail. Unfocused direction occurs when a business owner tries to do too many things at once, has unrealistic goals, or ignores basic business principles. Therefore, establish clear goals and create plans to achieve them, especially when starting out. This means you need a solid business plan and marketing foundation before launching your company.

Success is easy when you focus on business basics and direct your priorities!

Avoid the Squirrel Syndrome

It's not uncommon for a business owner or entrepreneur to spin their wheels and lose their focus. When this happens, many people start looking for the next bright, shiny object to grab hold of. This is called the Squirrel Syndrome.

- Squirrels have a severe inability to focus.
- Squirrels often dart back and forth—doubting their decisions—unable to choose a direction.
- Squirrels have something to teach us: what not to do.

The Squirrel Syndrome may cause abrupt dashes from one idea to another or one project to the next. When this happens, you become unfocused and may even become frantic about not getting things accomplished. The result is you delay or never complete important projects to reach your goals.

A good example of this unfocused reaction is how a dog reacts when seeing a squirrel. One of my favorite animated movies is the 2009 Pixar film *Up*. When Dug, the talking dog, meets his new friends, he is abruptly distracted when he thinks he sees a "Squirrel!"

Entrepreneurs can act a lot like Dug when they think they've found the next big idea or the next bright shiny object. The squirrels get in the way of focused productivity.

Most people can relate to the Squirrel Syndrome. That's why I throw stuffed squirrels into the audience at my live events to drive home the importance of staying focused. The squirrels serve as an anchor to remind the attendees to remain focused on business.

You can avoid Squirrel Syndrome by learning to recognize when a squirrel shows up in your life. Refocus by taking the time to define the project or direction in which you need to go. Then stay on task and turn off all distractions. No squirrels allowed! Revisit your vision to remain focused on what you most desire. Remember, every time you stray off course, it takes that much longer to reach your goals.

Pick a Path and Focus on the Future

Another way to avoid distractions is to learn how to say "no" to opportunities that do not serve your vision. Remain focused on results and move from one project to another in a timely fashion, always keeping your main goal in mind.

Far too many business owners and entrepreneurs don't have a clear, focused plan. And over time, their business pays the price. Without a clear direction, it's challenging to reach milestones and the final destination.

Successful people keep a laser-sharp focus on the future. This allows purposeful and significant contribution to building a higher level of success. By focusing on the future, you can better anticipate problems your company will face.

Focus on Activities That Create Results

Successful people develop habits that make success appear easy. Focus is one of those basic-but-critical, habits you need to master. Improve your focus on the day-to-day basic business activities you do best, and from which you produce extraordinary results. If you don't, you'll create higher stress levels and may experience burnout. When you spend most of your time and energy doing the business tasks you are brilliant at and allow others (like employees or subcontractors) to do the rest, you reap the biggest rewards.

For example, don't try building a website unless you're a webmaster, and don't try learning technical skills if that isn't the best use of your time. Outsource those things instead and focus on running your business so it can grow and prosper.

Learn how to focus on the big-picture projects that bring you the best results to gain the fastest and easiest success.

Mindful Multitasking

Not everyone can talk, email, and juggle at the same time. When you are focused and in the zone, you'll want to stay there as long as you can without distractions. When moving from one focus to another, you have to shift thinking, and it takes a while to get into the new zone or back into the previous one again. According to research done by Gloria Mark, who studies digital distraction at the University of

California, it takes approximately 23 minutes to return to the original task after an interruption. Therefore, even small interruptions can really add up throughout the day.

Running a successful business requires you to get good at avoiding distractions. Remaining focused in multiple directions isn't always easy. Not only can your focus change from activity to activity, it can also change from person to person, so you must deal with many factors, personalities, and unique styles of thinking.

The key to multitasking is to do it strategically and mindfully. Mindful multitasking means that you check in with yourself and determine where and how you need to focus in each new situation. For example, you focus differently in your car than at your desk or with family and friends.

Every situation requires a judgment call. Sometimes it's important to multitask and sometimes it isn't. Mindful multitasking allows you to stop reacting to distractions, such as the automatic reflex to answer the phone or read an incoming text. It allows you to focus on the actions that provide the best results and disregard everything else. After you set your intentions for the day (see Chapter 9 for more on this), create a to-do list that you can tackle using mindful multitasking, allowing yourself to be present in each action you take for the day.

Focus on Developing One Big Project at a Time

Do not try to start multiple projects at once. It fragments focus and time. Entrepreneurs are creative people, often with many good business ideas. And it's hard turning off the desire to act on multiple ideas at one time.

I know this because I have to fight it myself from time to time. But if you split your attention between more than one big project at a time, you'll run into trouble completing anything at all. You're going to need all your energy and focus to get your one new project off the ground.

Once your new business or project is up and running, it still needs your attention, even if you have gained some momentum and are excited to get creative with another idea. However, until you are stable and profitable, you are officially forbidden, based on my years of experience, to start another big project or business venture. Stay the course.

Here are five ways to help you remain focused on whatever your task at hand may be:

1. *Write out what you need to accomplish each day so you don't forget important tasks.* When a new idea comes to mind, don't stop what you're doing. Simply make a note of it and come back to it at a more convenient time.

2. *Focus on your overall ideas and then implement an effective action plan.* Keep your top three goals in mind and commit to achieving them each week. Write down the specific actions you need to take to achieve those goals.

3. *Tackle creative work first.* Mindless work will drain your energy, lower your focus, and waste your time. When you start with creative work at the beginning of the day, you can work on the most complex projects when your energy is highest before moving on to simpler tasks, such as answering emails or returning calls.

4. *Understand what is worthy of distraction.* Don't allow last-minute, nonemergency issues to kill your focus. Stay on task and stick to your commitments. Prioritize other tasks and put together a timeline so you're not needlessly distracted.

5. *Unplug from email, social media, and phone calls.* Take a break from all outside distractions and focus on the task at hand. You'll get a lot more done when you're not constantly interrupting yourself.

Focus on Your Motivation and Decisions

To fully enjoy your success, don't make money your sole driver. Think about the deeper reasons you want to become more successful. What is the real motivation that drives you toward success?

One of my clients, who had been a schoolteacher all her life, told me she was used to getting a paycheck. Now, as a new entrepreneur, she had to learn how to make money. She was more motivated than ever to go out there and make her own money—without limits.

As a business owner, you must focus on making money. If you don't make money, you either have a hobby, or you're out of business. But success is not only about making money. Money can buy a nice life, but it's easy to fall into the trap of believing that success, happiness, and wealth are all linked.

People often measure success by counting the zeroes in someone's salary or income. But if your life's ambition is just to make money, you're setting yourself up for frustration and disappointment. Money has to be a motivating factor, but it should not be your only goal for wanting more success.

Shameless, No-Nonsense Action Steps and Affirmation

Success Is Easy Affirmation (say it, believe it, and own it): "Success comes easy to me because I remain focused on business success, my goals, and who I can support in return."

1. *Focus on what works.* Good business practices are a mix of no-nonsense, practical experiences, good common sense, and the ability to foresee and prepare for the future. What you focus on will either move you forward or hold you back. Therefore, target what works and will make your success easy.
2. *Avoid Squirrel Syndrome.* Stay on task and get rid of all distractions. Every time you go off course, it takes you longer to reach your goals. Revisit your vision to remain focused on what you most desire.
3. *Focus on activities that create results.* Concentrate on the activities you do best and that produce the best return on your investment of time. Say "no" to opportunities that do not serve your vision. Remain focused on results and move from

one project to another in a timely fashion, always keeping your main goal top of mind.

4. *Work on only one big project at a time.* Multiple projects fragment your focus and time. Direct all your energy toward getting one new project off the ground. Once it is up and running, it still needs your attention, but at least you will have gained momentum. However, until you are stable and profitable, you are officially forbidden to start another big project or business venture.

5. *Focus on decisions that drive success.* To succeed, you must begin at the source of all choices, decisions, feelings, and experiences. To fully enjoy your success, don't use money as your sole motivator. Think about the deeper reasons you personally want to become more successful. Uncover the real motivation that drives you toward success, and you'll begin to gain real momentum that will have you making more money with ease.

SUCCESS IS EASY . . .
with Set Goals

There are many reasons to chase after goals, and people have different reasons at different times in their lives for pursuing them. You probably dream about your goals every day. Some days you move closer to achieving the success you desire. On other days, you might focus on the reasons why your dreams might not come true. But do you ever take the time to really think about why you desire success so much in the first place?

Let's focus on the latest success you have achieved to uncover the answer to this question. It doesn't have to be some huge achievement. A small success will do just fine. Imagine that achieving your success is like a journey; sometimes your journey can be quite easy, and sometimes it can be more challenging. Sometimes you arrive quickly, and other times it takes a long time to get there. Now think about why you took this journey in the first place and what helped you get there.

Where did your journey begin? Can you recall your emotions and experiences in that moment? Why did you decide to set this goal in the first place? How did you get started? Can you identify what motivated you to move forward? Were there obstacles along the way? What inspired you to move those obstacles out of the way and keep going until you reached your final destination?

How did you feel when you achieved your goal? Were you truly happy or somewhat disappointed?

Identifying why you want to achieve success is very important, because it's what will continue to motivate you to achieve future goals. Some of the reasons people are motivated to succeed include:

- Achieving goals brings up positive feelings because you know you are making positive progress.
- We love to win because achieving success is like a personal victory. Even when we fail along the way, we want to win in the end.
- Success stimulates our senses because it gives us purpose. The more challenging a goal, the stronger the feeling of success when we achieve it.
- Achievement challenges us to create bigger goals and excites us to continue to improve, both personally and professionally.
- Achieving success is often the solution to our problems. It allows more money, opportunity, and freedom to come our way.

In this chapter, you will not only discover how to achieve your goals, but you will also uncover why you want to achieve them and learn what will continue to drive you on your journey toward success.

What Motivates You to Achieve Your Goals?

What motivates you to succeed is something you need to discover for yourself. For most people, it is because success is strongly related to their life plan or mission. Some people love to win in business; others wish to get recognized for their personal accomplishments, and still others enjoy the challenges that come from going after bigger goals.

As for me, I started paying attention to reaching goals when I was ten years old and a friend of mine was wearing a Girl Scout uniform with a sash full of award badges. When I saw all those badges, my eyes lit up, and I got excited. The Girl Scouts uses badges to challenge young girls to explore new ideas and learn new skills. But back then, I just wanted to earn those darn badges so that I could show them off and get recognized for my accomplishments. This motivated me to do much more than the majority of the other girls. I was determined from that day forward to achieve every badge and fill up my uniform sash.

As an adult and business owner, my motivation to achieve my goals changed. Recognition was still important, but it was no longer a driving force. What motivated me more was the excitement and challenge of reaching new goals. For example, when I joined Toastmasters to learn how to become a better public speaker, I joined with the goal of getting my CTM (Competent Toastmaster) certification. After that, I was out of there and on to the next big challenge, which was to join the National Speakers Association (NSA) as a professional speaker. Then I wanted to achieve the level of CSP (Certified Speaking Professional). Less than 15 percent of NSA

Goals will drive you for different reasons at different times in your life.

members ever attain this. My motivation and driving force were to become the best of the best within my industry and to win in business.

People Who Set Goals Are More Successful

There are two kinds of people in business: those who have big goals and act on them, and those who say, "One day I'm going to . . ."

The first group is made up of planners and action takers. The second group is people who talk about making a plan and taking action, but never do. The difference between these two kinds of people is their level of commitment, energy, motivation, and drive to achieve goals.

Goal setting is the foundation for everything that follows, in both life and business. People who set goals are most successful in the long term. Most people do not successfully implement goal-setting strategies because they do not want to take the time to weigh the benefits, rewards and obstacles, or solutions and cost. So they just don't make any plans at all. If you keep targeting and tracking your goals, you will achieve far more than most of your competitors. And taking the steps outlined in this chapter makes success easy.

It's simply not enough to set and record goals. You must set the right kind of goals to succeed. Ideally, you want to set objectives that stretch your abilities and push you to learn new skills that generate more sales and income for your business.

Make a Firm Commitment to Your Goals

Goal setting is not just about creating a wish list. It's about making up your mind to firmly commit to a goal—enough to turn the goal into reality in your mind before it happens. That's the power of goal setting. Once you decide to set a big goal, go for it! Don't let anyone or anything get in the way. If for some reason your plan doesn't work as expected, change the plan, not the goal.

Choose to make every moment count. Every day is an opportunity to move toward your goals. Make the mental commitment that fear or doubt will motivate you rather than turning you aside. Accepting your fear can make it easy to rationalize abandoning your goals. Act despite your fear, and discover the outcome and consequences of your commitment.

Break Big Goals into Small Ones

One of the basic techniques of achieving your objectives is to break big goals into a number of small ones because nothing seems as difficult if it is broken down into smaller parts first. This dispels the overwhelming feeling you get when looking at the big picture. When you achieve short-range goals, the satisfaction you feel motivates you to move on to the next milestone.

Failure to understand this principle is what makes most people resist establishing large goals. Some people believe the effort involved in achieving big goals is too great. Or they are afraid about having to give up something by choosing to reach the goal.

To never make a decision is to never make a mistake. But indecisiveness creates frustration. When you refuse to decide, you experience self-doubt and inadequacy. But when you commit to your goals, you feel a tremendous surge of self-confidence and power. Knowing this, why not choose a big, worthy goal for yourself now? Successful people who achieve important goals rarely do so by accident; they make deliberate decisions that will move their business forward. They have a clear idea of what success looks and feels like, which serves as a goal-setting guide.

There isn't an unlimited amount of time or endless resources to devote to reaching your goals. You have to make the best use of the time and resources you have, so don't squander your energy and efforts. Make a firm commitment to move forward—and take steps every day to make it happen.

Take Consistent Action Steps Every Day

Looking at a big goal can be overwhelming. The key is to remember that goals are a combination of many small sub-goals. Any goal can be broken down into baby steps and then taken one step at a time.

If you're not achieving what you want, the first place to look is at your daily actions. What small steps are you taking every day toward your goal? You may be surprised to find that a daily action is missing or not consistent enough to produce your desired result. Every action you take contributes to your overall success. Nothing is too small or insignificant. If you're not getting the results you want, pay close attention to what you're not doing every day.

Define Your Goals with Clarity and Mission

Goal setting is about making choices. It is one of the key factors that will determine your success or failure. Said another way, if you don't know where you want to go, you'll probably end up someplace you don't want to be. Maybe you're at that place right now!

If you're not achieving what you're capable of, it's because your goals are not clearly defined. Goal setting gives you the courage to follow through and helps eliminate obstacles, distractions, and interruptions.

It also serves as a yardstick for progress. Where you put your focus is where your energy flows. When your energy flows in the right direction, you start to see results.

Goals are not wishes, but missions. You will not be 100 percent committed to a goal until you clearly define the benefits of the mission. This step becomes more and more important as you progress toward your destination and take on more challenging and complex goals.

If a written plan does not state the benefits, outcomes, and rewards that come with attaining a goal, you may become unmotivated when obstacles appear. That's why it's key to gain clarity on the end results.

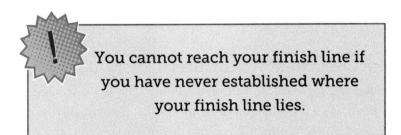

You cannot reach your finish line if you have never established where your finish line lies.

Don't Ignore Obstacles and Challenges

The biggest mistake most people make in goal setting is ignoring the inevitable obstacles and roadblocks. Success means making yourself aware of the goal's potential so you stay motivated.

As you become aware of these possible pitfalls, there is a tendency to become discouraged. But don't focus on the obstacles. Focus instead on how to overcome each one as it tries to get in the way of reaching your goals.

When obstacles appear, stop to reevaluate the benefits of moving forward until the goal outweighs the obstacles. This way, you'll feel more enthusiastic about removing any obstacle trying to hold you back. When a roadblock appears, concentrate on moving around it and toward the next step.

Use your overall goal as a point of reference, but concentrate on the individual steps it takes to get there. Even the largest, most challenging goals are attained one step at a time. Once you're aware of the obstacles, you will find that awareness alone will go a long way toward finding a solution.

Develop a Strategic Goal-Setting Plan

When you're clear about what you want, you can decide what activities and behaviors you need to achieve your goal. With time, your big goal will be broken down into smaller goals that direct you toward the finish line. Developing a strategic plan helps you schedule daily and monthly activities to reach that finish line with ease.

Developing a strategic plan might seem overwhelming at first, but when it's broken down, it's easy to manage. Here is a five-step approach to developing a strategic goal-setting plan.

1. *Determine where you are now and where you want to go.* Be realistic about how long it may take to achieve your goals. For example, if you're just beginning a new business, you'll need to plan time to develop your business and brand foundation before you implement sales and marketing tasks.

2. *Prioritize action steps and remain accountable.* Block out time on your schedule to review goals and think strategically about where you're headed each month. Brainstorm new ideas and strategies for growth by envisioning where you want to take the business long term. Hold yourself accountable for taking action.

3. *Define the expected objectives and benefits for each action.* Address only the main steps and priorities to move forward. Developing a strategic plan helps avoid wasted time and allows you to stop stressing about what to do next.

4. *Frequently review and reevaluate the strategic plan.* Review the action plans every quarter and the overall strategic plan annually. Putting together a detailed action plan a few months before each new year helps you stay ahead of business changes, reinvention, and strategic growth.

5. *Develop your company's core values.* Values and guiding principles help direct your decisions in everyday business. How you spend time, interact with others, and respond in business all comes down to your core values and personal beliefs. Core values work as a compass to keep you on course for the overall mission.

Strategic planning provides the structure to make day-to-day decisions that follow a larger vision. Planning strategically creates a direction for your business and maximizes your options for influencing your next steps. A strategic plan guides you toward your goal.

There is no wrong way to create a strategic plan. It doesn't have to be precise, and it can be adjusted over time, depending on the results you are producing. I suggest you focus on your biggest ROIs in time, money, and energy first, and then adjust your plan as needed. Of all the compelling reasons for you to engage in strategic planning, perhaps the most critical is the speed at which it forces you to choose a direction.

Strategic Planning Is Critical to Success

A strategic plan will help take your business to places you never thought possible. It will help keep your goals on track and focused on future success at all times.

Strategic thinking and planning comes naturally to me now. I love brainstorming and developing strategies for my clients. It's something I shine at because I enjoy the challenge of taking a big goal and breaking it down into smaller pieces. I approach the task with no-nonsense, common-sense strategies, manageable action steps, and a doable timeline, working backwards from the main goal to develop an achievable action plan. The strategy is based on other contributing factors surrounding my client's existing schedule, skill set, and ability to stay accountable and achieve results.

I like the brainstorming process to create new business ideas and innovative strategies. As I review the outcomes and benefits of my client's actions; we develop the action plan together, and I keep in mind a realistic timeline to achieve their goals.

How soon the client achieves their final goal is based on the starting point, consistency in taking action, and that realistic, achievable timeline. No matter the amount of strategy involved, it takes time to achieve a big goal. For example, when my client Ken started working to develop and grow a new speaking and consulting business, the first month he asked, "How soon can I quit my job? I'm working as fast as I can. I'm taking as much action as I can. When can I quit?"

As much as I wanted Ken to quit his job too, it was not realistic for him to plan on quitting in the near future. He first needed to put a timeline and a long-term strategic action plan in place. This included developing a business brand foundation, building a website, developing consulting programs, creating a marketing plan, and developing an online program. All these steps take months to position a client as the go-to expert in their niche market. They also need to learn new skills to help market and sell themselves to new clients.

So Ken and I developed very specific and strategic action steps. Once they were all in place, Ken started using his new skills to gain new clients and income-producing speaking engagements. Then his goals were to work on bigger strategic steps that would allow him to take that final step and finally quit his job. Those steps would help him reach his big vision and goals for launching a successful speaking and consulting business. Ken needed to make the same amount of income at his new business before quitting his day job.

Too many people jump into a new business without a strategic action plan in place and quit their day job too soon. This puts their business at risk of failure due to lack of direction, lack of planning, lack of skills, and ultimately lack of income.

Many of my clients think of strategic planning as a daunting task until I help break down the goals into manageable monthly action steps. The big goal or project may appear too overwhelming or challenging to address because the client simply doesn't know what smaller steps to take next.

Once the steps are laid out and broken down into manageable pieces, any size goal becomes easier to achieve. It's like putting all the puzzle pieces together to see the final picture.

Strategic thinking (brainstorming) and strategic planning (detailed goal setting) keeps your actions in line with your objectives at all times. With a strategic plan, you hold the keys to your success! How fun is that?

Shameless, No-Nonsense Action Steps and Affirmation

Success Is Easy Affirmation (say it, believe it, and own it): "Success comes easy to me because I have clearly-defined goals and remain committed to achieving these goals."

1. *Implement goal-setting strategies by weighing the benefits, rewards, obstacles, solutions, and cost.* Goal setting is the foundation for everything that follows. People who set goals are most successful long-term. Start out by discovering why

you want to achieve a goal. Then begin to write out a detailed plan stating the benefits, outcomes, and rewards for achieving your goals. Consider how you will feel once you've achieved your goals. Hold that feeling in your mind to drive you to action.

2. *Make a firm commitment to move forward and achieve your goals.* Discover what motivates you and drives you to action. Make the best use of the time and resources you have so you don't squander your energy and efforts. It's simply not enough to set and record your goals. You must set the right kind of goals to become more successful. The goal of every business owner is to set objectives that stretch your abilities and push you to learn new skills that generate more sales and income.

3. *Break big goals into smaller goals so you don't get over- whelmed.* Setting and achieving smaller goals gives you the motivation to follow through on bigger goals. This helps elimi- nate obstacles, distractions, and interruptions. It will also serve as a yardstick for your progress. You cannot reach your finish line if you have never established where it lies.

4. *Don't ignore the obstacles.* The biggest mistake you can make in goal setting is ignoring the obstacles and roadblocks. As you become more aware of possible pitfalls, there is a tendency to become discouraged and perhaps lose your enthusiasm. But don't focus on these obstacles—think about how to overcome each one as it tries to get in your way. When obstacles appear, stop to reevaluate the benefits of moving forward until the goal outweighs the difficulties. You'll feel more motivated to remove anything trying to hold you back. When a roadblock appears, concentrate on moving around it and toward the next step and the next and the next.

5. *Follow through on your goals with a strategic action plan.* Strategic planning will help keep your goals on track and keep you focused on future success at all times. When you are clear about what you want, you can decide what activities and

behaviors are required. With time, your big goal will be broken down into smaller goals that direct you toward the finish line. Developing a strategic plan helps you schedule daily and monthly activities so you can reach the larger goal with ease.

SUCCESS IS EASY . . .
with Strategic Action

I deas, preparation, knowledge, and courage are all but useless without action because action is the starting point of all progress. You must take positive action and make progress every day to succeed.

You don't need to get motivated to act. You can force yourself to take action, and motivation will follow. Action stimulates both the body and the brain. It brings you into contact with surprising things, unexpected events, and incredible people who have the potential to jump-start your success.

Think about it. You know how unmotivated you can get when you're just sitting around. It sure doesn't feel good when you haven't accomplished anything. Not taking action sets you back and makes you feel lazy!

Get into action, even if it's just to explore possibilities. You'll find that your creativity will rise to the occasion. Once that happens, you will become more motivated to take more action. Stay in motion, but remain flexible to change. You may not reach the original goal, but you might get guided to something even better. In either case, you will feel self-empowered and successful.

In this chapter, you will discover the power of taking consistent action and see how taking the right action at the right time brings you more long-term success. You will learn when it's time to hop on the opportunity train and when it's time to wait and concentrate on high-priority projects.

Having goals and a plan are not enough. You must commit to continually taking the right action!

Action Is the Key to Getting Things Done

Every action you take gets you one step closer to where you want to be. That's simply common sense, but it seems to be a challenge for a heck of a lot of people.

Unfortunately, actions you don't take don't count. Although you don't need to beat yourself up for what you don't do, it's really important to look at why. Ever wonder how different life might have ended up if you had actually done what you intended to do?

What got in your way? What stopped you from doing what you say you wanted to do?

Maybe you didn't want whatever it was badly enough, or maybe fear or doubt got in the way. Whatever stopped you from taking action also stopped you from having the success you wanted.

When you find yourself hesitating, figure out what is getting in the way and go around it, under it, or through it. Knock it over and keep going! Do whatever you need to do to get past what is stopping you. The longer you put off taking action, the longer you put off achieving success.

Also keep in mind that you can only succeed if you start somewhere—anywhere. To do that, you need to make strategic decisions. Most people are not good at this. For example, a lot of people want to start a business someday, but they keep putting off the decision while looking for the perfect business idea that will make millions of dollars. The main reason people postpone acting on their goals is lack of confidence.

To the degree you're not living your dreams, the limitations you set control you more than you control yourself. The only solution is to decide to start something. What may appear impossible can become possible—but only if you act!

Action Is the Secret to Manifesting the Life You Want

Actions allow you to create the life you want. Certainly some people have more natural talent in this area than others. But you can still learn to improve your ability to think and act strategically, and then manifest the success you want in life.

If there is a secret to manifesting what you want, it is this: the law of action. At times it doesn't even matter what you do as long as you do something. Action creates energy that generates movement, which creates more energy. Just like the laws of motion, the law of action is a universal law. In fact, they must work hand in hand because one won't work without the other.

Newton's third law of motion says that for every action, there is an equal and opposite reaction. Energy is constantly in motion, therefore every action you take must have a reaction. Energy is never created nor destroyed, but is constantly changing. Therefore, everything you do has some sort of reaction. You can apply the same concept to success.

This doesn't mean you can just envision a successful life and suddenly it magically happens. It doesn't work like that. The universe will not just provide for you unless you supply the energy to move it into action. It only knows how to react, which means you must do more than think about what you want. You must take your ideas and put them into action. You must get off your butt and take some real kick-ass action to manifest results now! What you do creates the momentum to help get what you want.

This is the no-nonsense reality. I know it's true because I've seen the results myself. When I put these two laws to work for me, I'm rewarded with success in return. Any time I've tested either one with lack of momentum or action on my part, results slowed or stopped without fail. The law of action is the secret to manifesting results!

An Action Plan Keeps You in Motion

To move forward, you'll need a concise action plan with a detailed, step-by-step road map. You don't drive a car without knowing where you're going. Instead, you decide where you're headed and why, and then you figure out which route you'll take. You then take additional steps to decide what time to leave and what time to arrive. Every part of the road trip is planned out in advance.

The same attention to detail should happen when you create a road map to follow in business. An action plan keeps you in motion and helps you make day-to-day decisions on the road toward your goals. This, in turn, guides you to maximize your chances for thriving in business.

Take the Right Action to Achieve Long-Term Success

Your actions should focus on the highest-priority projects in your business at all times. Every day you make choices, either to do what is most important, or to do something less significant. When you find yourself spending time on tasks that have little to do with your main objective, ask, "Why am I doing this?"

One of the biggest complaints people have is lack of time. But the real issue is lack of clarity on what action to take and the benefits of that action. If you aren't clear on that, it's challenging to get started. So be very specific and detail-oriented when it comes to creating your road map, and choose your action items wisely.

Act Despite Fear

Even successful, confident people are afraid of making changes and trying new things. The difference between successful people and unsuccessful ones is that successful people act in spite of their fear. They feel the fear and move past it. Moving past your fear allows you to feel more courageous.

Courage gives you the wisdom to act in spite of fear. Wisdom provides the discernment to make good decisions. Courage and wisdom move you beyond your limitation zone toward new actions with ease. Successful people know this. You know it, too, so as you create your action plan, account for your own "fear factor" and make plans to overcome it as you move toward success.

> **Don't ever stop taking action just because you fear you may fail.**

Hop on the Opportunity Train

Your action plan is useless if you don't take advantage of opportunities to grow your business. The Opportunity Train is pulling into the station. It has very limited seating and will be leaving shortly. Who gets on the train? Only decisive, successful people who are ready to take quick action get a seat on the train.

Who's left behind? Indecisive people who are too afraid to move or take action—these people miss out. The train leaves the station without them. Unsuccessful people fail to act for fear of making a mistake. And this failure causes them to miss the train day after day.

Daily action or inaction is your responsibility! Get into action, because the train is waiting! Make the decision to hop on the Opportunity Train when it shows up, and be willing to pay the price for the ticket.

Prioritize Actions and Build Your Business

Having a goal and a sense of clarity are not enough to succeed. You must have the courage to take action and react promptly when good opportunities appear. You can often have so many important projects to accomplish that it's difficult to figure out which ones to tackle first. You could become overwhelmed and end up doing nothing. Or you could pick the wrong project focus and end up wasting valuable time and energy.

For example, it's not unusual for me to meet people who start writing a book before they have a business plan to back it up. Why would someone spend countless hours writing a book hoping it succeeds when they have no plan to achieve it? That's simply crazy! But a lot of people hope a book will succeed the hard way. Common sense proves otherwise.

To succeed at any business venture, you can't put the cart before the horse if you want success to come easily. Let's talk about some steps you can take to make sure you do things right.

Concentrate on High-Priority Projects

To make better progress toward achieving success, concentrate exclusively on the highest-priority projects that produce the most beneficial results. Once you achieve results from these top-priority projects, you will reap the rewards in the form of more customers, income, etc.

For example, one of the high-priority strategies I teach business owners is to create what I call the Quick Cash Formula.

This concept includes coming up with an idea for a new service or package of services to generate quick income for the business. Once you develop an offer, make a presentation to your existing customers or existing network (these people are the easiest to sell to). This group is your loyal following, and they are often waiting for any new offer or special you provide to quickly invest in. Existing customers already love working with you and want more of the services or products you have to offer. Quick cash and income flow into your business when you prioritize this strategy.

Use Strategic Action to Prioritize Results

It takes self-disciplined action to achieve meaningful results. Make strategic choices to act in accordance with your long-term success rather than seeking instant gratification. This takes disciplined, organized action and future-oriented thinking or strategic thinking— day-to-day implementation of strategic action that determines where you stand at the end of a week, a month, a year, or even a lifetime. You can't afford to sit back and passively allow the future to catch up with you. You must prepare to think and act strategically.

That's what I do. People often say to me, "How do you get so much done?"

That's easy: I'm always prioritizing my actions and thinking ahead. I do three things every day that move me toward my main

Stop wasting your time on projects that don't get big results. Take strategic action that moves you directly toward your main goal!

goal. The rest of my action items either get moved to another day or delegated to my team, whom I trust to get things done effectively.

To work more strategically, collect your thoughts and implement an action plan. This helps you stay on track with priorities. Determine the top three action steps you need to do today to help stay focused on your main goal for tomorrow. Identify what specific actions you need to take that will help you gain traction and momentum.

Avoid Perfectionism

Preparation is a good thing, but over preparation caused by perfectionism is costly. There's a fine line between being well prepared and over prepared. In extreme cases, an obsession with perfection can negate your efforts toward beneficial action altogether.

In the business world, perfection is more likely to inhibit your chances of success than increase them. Perfectionism will create more roadblocks, obstacles, and setbacks in the long run. It will cause you to waste valuable time and overlook success opportunities. You'll spend too much time planning and perfecting before launching a business or project.

Even worse, perfectionism can make you feel crushed when you fail because of your extremely high standards and unrealistic expectations for success. This creates stress, which takes a toll on the creative and productive energy you should use for more beneficial projects.

At its extreme, perfectionism can turn into a phobia of failure and making mistakes. These fears stop the perfectionist from taking action, so they don't make progress or have much success in business. Want to succeed? Stop trying to be perfect. It's never a goal you can achieve.

Excellence in Business Does Not Require Perfection

While it's sometimes possible to benefit from striving for perfection, these exceptions to the rule are very few and far between. That's why they're called "exceptions." Spending too much time perfecting one small area of your business isn't good business sense.

In business, you often need to go with what you've got and move on instead of trying to achieve perfection. This doesn't mean you should accept mediocrity. It means thinking in terms of "It's good enough for now."

EVERYONE PROCRASTINATES

We all have a tendency to procrastinate when it comes to doing things we don't enjoy. For example, I put off doing my taxes until the last minute every year because I consider it "work." But when I finally complete them, I always feel relieved once I check it off my list and put it behind me.

Every year I promise myself, "Next year will be different. I'll get my taxes done early." But when next year rolls around, the same procrastination causes the same painful process.

Procrastinators are often smart, capable, hardworking people who still can't get things done on time and can't seem to figure out why. If you are wondering about the "why" behind procrastination, take a look at the questions below to gain some insight:

- When you are faced with a project that feels uncomfortable, are you focusing on what could go wrong? If so, why?

- Do you ever feel overwhelmed by the responsibility of your actions? If so, why?

- Do you believe that you're going to have to do something perfectly? If so, why?

- Do you have anxiety or stress because you don't hold yourself accountable for taking action? If so, why?

While there are many reasons for procrastination, the results are often the same. They come down to avoidance and lack of accountability and then a feeling of guilt that you let yourself and others down by not delivering what you promised.

Some people procrastinate because of their fear of success. They find it easier to talk about success than try to achieve it, so they procrastinate as a way of life.

For example, a gentleman who had attended my Highly Paid Expert Workshop a few times came up to me at a recent event and said, "I really want to become a successful speaker like you. I've

---

EVERYONE PROCRASTINATES, continued

been following you and other successful professionals for years. I've attended events and taken lots of notes, but I can't seem to make it happen for myself. Why do you think that is?"

I replied, "Only you know the answer to that question. It's in your head. You have been surrounded by the masters to guide you for years. The teachers have appeared, but the student won't take action. Only you know what's stopping you from taking action and moving forward!"

He responded, "Wow, that's so insightful. You're right. No one has ever told me that before."

Insightful? Really? This seems like simple common sense.

It didn't surprise me that when he left the event that weekend, he took no action toward his goal. I'm going to assume that he will continue to procrastinate and will most likely never achieve his dream of becoming a successful speaker. He will also continue to lie to himself and everyone else that he wants to succeed. Procrastination may be common, but it doesn't have to win the day. Get over it and get on with your action plan!

Feeling Stuck Makes You Feel Overwhelmed

Success requires you to be honest with yourself about why you don't take action when you say achieving your dreams is what you want most in life.

Some people think it's safer to remain in their comfort zone doing the things they already know how to do. But that is not the easy way out, and it's certainly not success! Staying in your comfort zone is living a boring, stuck life.

You can't possibly grow personally, expand your knowledge, and take action that empowers you when you're stuck. Remaining stuck is a vicious cycle that leads to feelings of being undervalued and underappreciated. It also makes some people feel overwhelmed.

Many people feel overwhelmed with busywork that gives the appearance of working hard toward success. If you're busy, then you're achieving goals, right? But the busywork is really causing you to delay taking serious action for success.

That seems crazy! Why would someone work so hard to avoid becoming successful?

There are many reasons, but most likely it boils down to self-sabotage due to the fear of failure. Ironically, by not even trying, the person is failing anyway.

It's important to be aware of how serious you are about taking the right strategic action steps to succeed without feeling overwhelmed. With that awareness, you will know when you subconsciously stop yourself from taking action toward success. You will realize when you are making success harder than necessary. And why do that when it can become easy for you?

Awareness is the first step toward becoming honest with yourself. When you are aware, you can shift focus to something that your mind perceives as doable and gain results. When you get into a productive mode, you increase your positive energy, direction, and motivation, and those feelings of being overwhelmed will go away. As you gain focus and start to see results from your actions, you will gain the courage to take bolder actions, which drive you to more challenging projects and bigger results!

Build Your Bold-Action Momentum

What bold action would you take if you were part of an experiment, if there was no judgment, and if you knew you couldn't fail?

To get started, imagine taking bold steps in your mind. The more you practice, the easier it will be to take action in real life. The bolder you feel and believe you are, the easier it becomes to take bold action and increase your momentum toward success.

Don't be afraid to shock yourself with bold action! If you couldn't fail, what bold action would you take now?

As you begin to identify those bold action steps in your mind, how does it make you feel? Do you feel more confident and empowered? Will bold action move you closer to your big vision?

Having a big vision is vital, but it's only the first step on the path to achieving success. Vision will direct you and give you focus, but taking bold action will create a powerful impact! As such, bold ideas lead to bold action, which in turn releases your shameless success potential. You cannot realize your unlimited potential until you take bold action. When you do, you enter a higher state of awareness, which provides the solutions you need to eliminate your problems and accomplish your objectives.

Anything you do, so long as it is purposeful and constructive, is considered productive action. The greatest expansion of your mental paradigm comes from taking bold action. When new opportunities don't seem to come your way with ease, it's time to try some bold action to gain results.

As you start to enjoy shameless success from making bold moves, your confidence and personal power will soar, allowing you to take even bigger and bolder steps. The bigger the goal, the bolder the action you need to take. In return, you'll be rewarded with bigger achievements and a higher level of success. Don't be afraid to become bolder!

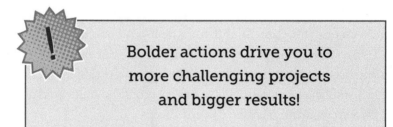

Bolder actions drive you to more challenging projects and bigger results!

Do It, Delegate It, Get It Done

Sometimes you need help to build your bold-action momentum. There are some tasks that you can (and should) do yourself. But if the task is small and unimportant, delegate it. Good delegation involves the willingness to let go. Learning how to delegate helps you leverage your work and multiply your action.

Delegation allows you to move from what you can do yourself to what you can manage. It's an important business skill to learn, especially as your company grows. Without the ability to delegate effectively, it is impossible for you to achieve a higher level of success.

Do it. Delegate it. Either way: Get it done!

Shameless, No-Nonsense Action Steps and Affirmation

Success Is Easy Affirmation (say it, believe it, and own it): "Success comes easy to me because I have strategic and bold action to keep me achieving more."

1. *Force yourself to take action and motivation will follow.* Get into action, even if it's just to explore possibilities. Your creative ideas will rise to the occasion. Remember that every action gets you one step closer to where you want to be.

2. *Create a concise action plan with a detailed road map.* An action plan keeps you in motion and helps you make decisions on the road toward your goals. It takes self-disciplined action to achieve meaningful results. Make strategic choices to act in accordance with your long-term success instead of acting to achieve instant gratification. This will take disciplined, organized action and require future-oriented thinking. It involves day-to-day implementation of strategic action that determines where you stand at the end of a week, a month, a year, or even a lifetime.

3. *Prioritize actions as you build your business.* You must have the courage to act and react when good opportunities appear. Stop wasting your time on projects that don't get big results. Take strategic action that moves you directly toward your main goal! To make better progress, concentrate exclusively on your highest-priority projects that will produce the most-beneficial results first. Once you achieve results from your top-priority projects, you will reap the rewards in the form of more customers, more sales, and more income.

4. *Avoid perfectionism.* Preparing is a good thing, but over preparation is costly when you try to be perfect. Perfectionism can be a destructive path that will create more roadblocks, obstacles, and setbacks in the long run. It will cause you to waste valuable time and overlook success opportunities. Worse, it can make you feel crushed when you fail due to extremely high standards and unrealistic expectations for success.

5. *Practice taking bold action steps.* The more you practice, the easier it is to take bold action. What bold action would you take if it were an experiment and you couldn't fail? The bigger your goal, the bolder your action plan needs to be. The bolder you feel and believe you are, the easier it is to build momentum. Don't be afraid to take bold action to achieve what you most desire. It's time for you to boldly go for it!

SUCCESS IS EASY ...
with Calculated Risks

Taking risks can be frightening. Everything you do in life involves risk. Even doing nothing is risky. Life without risk is simply not an option.

There is no perfect way to take a risk. You may decide to plunge forward recklessly or tiptoe in cautiously. Neither way is right or wrong, but if you creep forward at a snail's speed, you might miss out on a great opportunity. Everyone has opportunities, but the most successful people view them much more clearly and take action even when there is risk.

People achieve, surpass, and succeed in business because they dare to live beyond the realm of what's considered "normal." These people have learned the art and skill of risk taking.

In this chapter, you will learn what stops most people from taking risks and discover why playing it safe in business is a deadly success killer.

What Stops People from Taking Risks

People who are uncomfortable taking risks will often exaggerate the consequences of failure. Even when setting the odds correctly, they often tend to overestimate the negatives. When this happens, you might picture unrealistic worst-case scenarios and assume the risk will produce negative results.

It's not uncommon to underestimate your ability to handle the consequences of risk. In reality, something bad could happen, but in most cases, it's probably something you can handle. When you understand how to focus on the calculated risks while eliminating the risks that go along with poor planning, you will have no trouble taking on more calculated risks.

Most people don't reach the level of success they dream of achieving due to their fear of taking risks and living beyond their boundaries. They decide to play it safe. Rarely do you hear warnings about playing it safe in business and in life. Playing it safe causes more loss in the long run. Avoid it at all costs!

Playing It Safe Is a Silent Killer of Success

Refusing to take risks is a slow, silent killer of success. Not taking risks may become more dangerous than ambitious risk taking, because you don't realize the results until you are stuck and don't know why.

First, you must understand the dangers of playing it safe. While it may feel better in the short term, it's risky for your long-term results. This false sense of security has a tendency to sneak up on you because the danger often lurks under the surface.

The solution to playing it safe is easy. Start by asking yourself questions about how you can do business differently. Consider these questions to find what makes you feel overly comfortable when it comes to playing it safe:

- Why would you settle for getting by when you can have more success?
- What good opportunities have slipped by you in the past because you didn't take a risk?
- How would taking on more risk make your business more successful?

To get better at taking risks, first conduct the research and analyze the risks; then you can move into action. This will give you the confidence you need to take more calculated risks with ease.

Analyze Your Risk

Every decision you make in business has some level of risk attached to it. To grow a business, you must open yourself up to taking on more risks, even small ones. Calculated risks can be very rewarding as part of a thought-out, detailed business plan. Don't dwell on the decision or overanalyze it. Always consider the risk/reward ratio.

Keep in mind that without risk, there is no reward. In reality, the chances of something not working out are often much lower than you think. Don't be afraid to boldly go where you've never gone before. Focus on the opportunity and evaluate the potential rewards and outcomes before making an informed decision. Weigh in on the possible outcomes by asking yourself:

- What's the best-case scenario?
- What's the worst-case scenario?
- What's the most likely scenario?

Try to create a realistic balance between these three scenarios. To do this, you'll need to weigh the odds and calculate the balance between the risk and the reward to decide if it's worth taking the risk. Consider the worst-case scenario by asking these questions:

- What's the worst that can happen?
- If the worst did happen, how could it affect business?
- Is it still worth taking the risk if things don't go just right?
- Does the reward outweigh the risk?

Most of the time the worst never happens, especially when you're well-prepared. Still, considering how to deal with it will make it easier for you to decide whether to take the risk.

For example, you risk missing out on a sale because you believe your prospect may reject your offer. In the worst-case scenario, a fierce competitor keeps getting the sales instead, you miss out on a lot of income, and you eventually go out of business. But that's not likely to happen if you continue to improve your sales skills. What is more likely is that you ask your prospect one more time, and they agree to do business with you, creating a big sale and a huge windfall for your business. And the most likely scenario is that you will continue to sell to some prospects and miss out on others. Your odds will continue to improve as you strengthen your sales skills, and your income will rise along with your sales.

CONSIDERING MY OWN WORST-CASE SCENARIO

When I was thinking about starting my own world speaking tour, I had to consider the worst-case scenario when calculating the risk. The worst-case was that it could cost me thousands of dollars in lost income by not being able to fill seats and making sales in an area that I had no following. Yet I still I wanted to give it a try because building an international following was my goal.

First, I needed to decide where to begin the tour. I chose New Zealand because I had always wanted to travel there for an extended period of time.

I balanced the risks and the rewards in my mind and decided it was worth going for. The reward was an amazing month-long adventure around New Zealand. The risk was a very costly trip and valuable time away from my business. Another risk I needed to weigh was that if I didn't try to launch my world speaking tour now, then when? I might get discouraged and never take the risk in the future.

....

CONSIDERING MY OWN WORST-CASE SCENARIO, continued

The fear of missing out (FOMO) on an exciting opportunity was my deciding factor, and I moved into action. I picked the initial seminar date and started looking for a hotel to host my event in Auckland, New Zealand. I gave myself six months from the planning date to secure other speaking engagements around the country to help me fill the seats for my two-day seminar.

Next I booked a flight to Auckland for a week to finalize the seminar location. I remember my hands shaking as I signed the contract for the hotel ballroom rental. It was scary to rent a large room with no database or following in that part of the world to fill it.

During this first visit, I met a couple of meeting planners and asked if I could get booked to speak to their groups in exchange for a seminar sponsorship. This gave me a chance to sell tickets for my own event, and the meeting planners were thrilled to gain a high-level business speaker from America. It was a win for the planners, the audience, and me!

Before the tour began, I booked a few more speaking engagements, which helped me feel confident that my risk was worth chasing. A few months later, I was ready to head off on my exciting new adventure. I traveled the North and South Islands of New Zealand, sightseeing and speaking along the way, before heading back to Auckland to present my seminar. My assistant, Kathy, flew in from Arizona to help with the event. I even had a sponsor fly in from the United States to build her international following for a direct-sale business.

My very first international seminar was about to begin, and the ballroom was full of business owners and entrepreneurs I had met along my journey. It was a success! This was just the first seminar of dozens in 27 more countries on my three-year world tour. My calculated risk paid off for me many times over.

....

Taking a Calculated Risk vs. a Crazy Risk

Not all risks are created equal. There is a big difference between a well-thought-out, calculated risk and a poorly planned, crazy risk. A crazy risk is one that you act on without regard for the possible consequences.

A crazy risk could deliver a positive return, but the problem is you entered into it blindly without knowing the rewards. This is a dangerous gamble to make.

A calculated risk, on the other hand, involves advance research and detailed planning. The results aren't guaranteed to be positive, but at least you've done enough due diligence to increase your chances of success.

Instead of taking every chance that comes along, learn to make smart decisions and smart moves. Decide what is a calculated risk and what is a crazy risk when it comes to business. When trying to figure out your plan, ask yourself the following questions:

- On a scale from 1 to 10, with 1 being no risk and 10 being a crazy risk, what level of action are you willing to take, considering the risk/reward ratio? Consider how to take on more calculated risks while avoiding a crazy blind leap of faith.

- Can you live with the consequences of the worst-case scenario? If you can't handle a negative outcome, the risk is probably too crazy. Rethink the risks and the rewards so that any possible negative results are downgraded to something you can deal with.

- Have you researched the risk you want to take in detail? Learning how to "look before you leap" will help build confidence and make the risk more calculated.

- Will you lie awake at night worrying that you may have missed out on a great opportunity by not taking a risk? Or will you lie awake worried because taking the risk is causing you too much stress? Only you can decide if the risk is worth it.

- Are you willing to take action even if you are afraid? Fear is a natural byproduct of risk-taking. You need to get comfortable with your own fear threshold.

- Have you asked for help from a consultant or business associate to gain a new perspective on the risk? Get feedback from supportive action takers who will help you consider other perspectives and options and the risk/reward ratio before you take action.

Evaluate Your Risk/Reward Ratio

To increase your chances of only taking on risks with the potential for high returns, keep the following tips in mind:

- *Evaluate the risk/reward ratio by doing research in advance.* To take a calculated risk, understand every detail and angle of the decision. This will help you see any red flags and possible challenges ahead of time.
- *Anticipate mistakes and obstacles when considering your risk.* Account for each of these in advance. Before deciding, consider the positive outcomes and rewards in multiple directions. Also think about potential mistakes or obstacles that could arise. Finally, consider if there is another direction or action you should take instead.
- *Identify long-term goals and implement checkpoints along the way.* Your end goal may be months or years away, so plan how to stay on course and keep motivated from start to finish. Also think about how to implement checkpoints along the way to keep your focus on your long-term goals. These will help you identify if the calculated risk is worth chasing after or if it will take too much attention to detail, time, and money.
- *Get ready to make changes to the risk-taking action plan.* Unfortunately, a business decision rarely, if ever, goes as planned, so stay alert to necessary adjustments along the way. Change may require you to go in another direction, handle a different problem, or find a new solution. Be willing and ready to make a shift if or when things don't go as planned. You can't always control the results, but you can always control how you respond.

As you get increasingly comfortable with taking on more risk, remember that every risk is different, yet every risk is the same. You need to have some fundamentals in place before you take the leap, but not too many. Keep in mind that it wouldn't be a risk if you knew everything that was about to happen, would it?

Say "Yes" Only to Risks Worth Taking!

You can't say "yes" to every opportunity that comes along. Learn how to say "no" to opportunities that don't serve your personal goals. Below are three tips to help you understand which opportunities to walk away from:

1. *Say "yes" to well-calculated risks and "no" to outrageous risks.* Part of the anxiety that drives us when seeking out new opportunities is the sense of finality about it all. There's this fear that if you go for it, you're stuck whether you like it or not. Those are pretty high stakes, so the temptation to say "no" makes sense. But saying "yes" allows you to flex your muscles a little and free yourself to try something new. You can always adjust it later if it doesn't work out. It's that easy! When you acquire this skill of saying "yes" to new opportunities, success will soon follow.

2. *Say "no" when business gets too risky.* Risk taking is both an art form and a learned skill, and so is knowing when to say "yes or "no" to the right opportunities. Sometimes you'll need to trust your instinct, or gut feeling, when you feel that a risk just isn't right for you, even if the risk serves your goals. For example, if there is a possible business relationship at risk or a legal risk that could backfire on your business—avoid taking the chance.

3. *Call for reinforcements when you just don't have the answer.* Risks can be scary and cause us to doubt our direction. It's the not knowing what will happen next that's truly frightening. Sometimes the only way to feel comfortable making a decision is to discuss it with another successful person who has already learned from their own experience. Lessons from their own risk taking situations may help teach you how to tackle your own challenging decision.

Successful entrepreneurs are willing to take on a lot of risk. They've learned that although they may feel a bit scared or anxious whenever risky decisions arise, it doesn't hold them back. Risk taking is just part of the success equation. Therefore, the next time you feel scared about taking risks, just think of it as another great experience.

Be brave and take on risk. Nothing can substitute for your own experiences!

> You can't grow in business if you are unwilling to take risks, push the boundaries, and take a bold stand for success!

Shameless, No-Nonsense Action Steps and Affirmation

Success Is Easy Affirmation (say it, believe it, and own it): "Success comes easy to me because I have learned to take calculated risks to keep growing and expanding my business."

1. *Refuse to play it safe.* Playing it safe is a silent killer of success. Learn to take more calculated risks with proven strategies. Keep in mind that without risk there is no reward. Understand that there are risks to playing it safe, too. While playing it safe may feel better in the short term, it's dangerous to long-term results. This false sense of security has a tendency to sneak up on you because the danger often lurks under the surface. The solution to playing it safe is easy: Start by asking yourself challenging questions about how to do business differently.

2. *Consider the worst-case and best-case scenarios when deciding if it's worth taking a risk.* When you consider the worst-case scenario first, the decision about whether to take the risk becomes easier. As you take on more risk, remember that every risk is different, yet the same. You need to have some fundamentals ready before you take the leap, but not too many.

Keep in mind that it wouldn't be a risk if you knew everything that was about to happen, would it?

3. *Learn how to make smart decisions and smart moves when it comes to risk taking.* Decide what is a calculated risk or a crazy risk. A crazy risk *could* deliver a positive return, but you may enter into it blindly not knowing the results. This is a dangerous gamble to make. A calculated risk, on the other hand, involves advance research and detailed planning. The results aren't guaranteed, but at least you've done enough due diligence to increase your chances of succeeding.

4. *Evaluate the risk/reward ratio.* Before taking a calculated risk, understand every detail and angle of the decision. This gives you time to spot any red flags or possible challenges in advance. On a scale from 1 to 10, with 1 being no risk and 10 being a crazy risk, what level of action are you willing to take, considering the risk/reward ratio? Consider how to take on more calculated risks while avoiding a crazy blind leap of faith.

5. *Say "yes" to only the risks worth taking.* Learn how to say "no" to opportunities that don't serve your personal goals. Walk away from opportunities that don't give you a high probability of success. When you take risks, you must anticipate potential mistakes and obstacles. Account for each of these in advance. Before executing any decision, consider the possible outcomes and the rewards in multiple directions, and ask yourself if there is another direction or action you should take instead. Identify long-term goals and implement checkpoints along the way. The end goal of your risk may be months or years away, so plan to stay the course and remain motivated until the final result.

commitment to excellence and growth

14

SUCCESS IS EASY . . .
with a Plan
for Growth

S uccess is a continuous journey. It takes time and planning to grow a successful business. With only half of startup companies surviving more than five years, you must ensure your business is sustainable for the long haul. The best way to do that is to create a growth plan.

Planning for growth involves more than a vision for long-term success. The key is to develop a consistent plan by looking at competitors, focusing on your strengths, and investing in changing market conditions.

As your business grows, you must grow along with it, making better strategic decisions and working on the business rather than working in the business.

Most people want their business to keep improving, yet they value peace and stability over growth and change. You can't improve and remain the same. Growth requires change. Change means challenging the status quo. If you want greater growths, you can't settle for what you have now. The only time you grow is when you are uncomfortable.

In this chapter, you will discover that success is a continuous journey toward future growth. Yet it's easy with guidance from accountability partners, mentors, or mastermind groups that can help you level up your skills.

Achieve Your Growth Potential with Accountability

I believe almost anything is possible with the right plan and action steps to support it, but you must engage in some form of accountability to ensure success, or you will fail. Success is easy when you have someone to help you stay accountable.

It's important to find a business consultant who can provide the accountability, critical thinking, and strategic planning you need to encourage you toward a plan for continued growth. When you are held accountable, you are forced to expand and grow, setting you up to believe in greater possibilities.

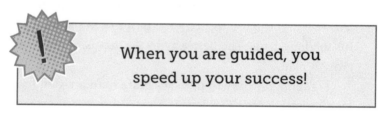

When you are guided, you speed up your success!

Connect with mentors and business consultants who can expand your vision for growth. Remain coachable, open, and willing to ask for help. Asking others to guide you is not a weakness. It's a requirement if you want to grow your business to the next level.

Never Stop Seeking Out Advice

I grew up knowing nothing about success. I got poor grades in high school and was lucky to graduate. But I was smart enough to know when to shamelessly ask for help whenever I found someone who could guide me toward success. I found the right people, who taught me or connected me to someone else who could. I never gave up seeking advice and looking for mentors, and I never stopped growing. Even to this day, I continue to hire mentors to support my success.

My mentors are my business and life "professors." Some of the greatest success authorities in the United States, highly successful entrepreneurs themselves, showed me that success is easy. Having these mentors share their most treasured secrets to help me grow and prosper in business was as good as getting multiple master's degrees from universities. The unique lessons I learned about how to succeed much faster helped me sharpen my skills and strategies in every aspect of business.

This guidance helped me graduate from the University of Hard Knocks, where I learned the skills of building and growing a business in the trenches. Anytime I wanted to learn, I found someone to guide me and get me there faster.

Having a mentor is like taking a secret shortcut to success. And although it's the best way to grow, most people don't find a guide, consultant, or mentor for help. Know this: You can't do it alone, whatever it is. You must find a highly successful person to guide you. Invest in success now by finding a mentor for support. It's an easy fast tract to success.

I've always found brilliant guides and mentors. I've learned more from some than from others, but I learned something useful from everyone I've invested in. Even at the start, when I didn't have much to offer in return, I always had enthusiasm and was a sponge for learning about success. These people took me under their wings and allowed me to fly with them.

Decide if You're a Business Owner or an Entrepreneur

When it comes to deciding on your growth plan, think about what kind of business owner you are. There's often confusion between the terms "business owner" and "entrepreneur." Both run businesses, but they have divergent styles of leadership and thoughts on running the business, which means they have different outlooks on growth.

Business owners focus more on a consistent weekly and monthly schedule instead of a long-term, bigger outcome for the company. It's important to them to know what's coming next, so they can make calculated decisions resulting in a clear and steady outcome. This strategy does not often result in huge growth, but it keeps the business moving forward. They focus on gaining new customers and making more sales to grow the business without considering selling or duplicating it from the start. Business owners often start their company to create a steady job and income, and often stay busy trying to do it all instead of doing the things that help the business grow.

A TRUE ENTREPRENEUR AT HEART

When I bought into the family car rental business at the age of 19, I was excited to call myself a new business owner. At the time, I wanted to build something successful and create more income for the business and myself. I never thought about building it to sell. In fact, my brother owned the same car rental business for 50 years before he sold it.

Before I left the car rental business, we built and sold another business within the same company, which taught me to consider a build-to-sell model from the start. When I left to open my first retail clothing store, I thought of myself as a business owner, but my vision was to grow the business as an entrepreneur. My plan was to develop a strong team so I had time

A TRUE ENTREPRENEUR AT HEART, continued

away from the business to expand into another location. This eventually led me to sell all my retail locations and move on to the next chapter in my entrepreneurial life.

I'm a true entrepreneur at heart! I love the process of building and growing a business. I enjoy the challenge of developing something from an idea to a success. Once I get things dialed in and running, I'm usually off looking for a new project. That doesn't mean I leave the business behind—by the time I'm ready to move on, that business is running by itself with my team supporting it. Or it becomes one of my multiple income streams.

My current one-page business plan includes developing multiple income streams, which are all based around the same business model. My business is professional speaking and consulting. From those two areas, I host my own workshops, specialty master classes, client VIP days, online courses, professional keynote speaking, and business mentoring. I handle all these income streams under one roof and still maintain a financially independent lifestyle while working about 40 hours a week.

My business plan allows me to stay busy, make a great income, and still have time off when I want and work anywhere in the world I choose.

I'm never without a new project or a new income stream to develop. But any new project must fit into my existing core business model as an additional income stream—not a completely different project far outside the scope of my expertise.

Most important, I always live by the motto, "If it's not fun, I'm not doing it anymore." In other words, if it's not challenging me, I move on to the next project—living my life as a true entrepreneur.

Entrepreneurs have big ideas and are more open to taking risks, even when the ideas aren't proven. They often jump in with both feet, not knowing whether their efforts will pay off. Most entrepreneurs think months and years ahead, focusing on the long-term future of the business and aiming for huge growth. They are either focused on ultimately selling the business or developing it to run without needing them to be on-site. The entrepreneurial model is either build to sell or build to magnify, with multiple locations and/or multiple income streams.

Do you consider yourself a business owner or an entrepreneur— or a little of both?

One is not necessarily better than the other when it comes to success; they're just different. It's important to know where you fit in when defining your success.

So think long and hard about which kind of business owner you are. Doing so will inform your plans for growth and scale down the road.

Growth Depends on Your Degree of Freedom

There are varying degrees of freedom in business. For example, solopreneurs have a certain amount of freedom to run their business as they wish. They may walk away from a full-time job to create a business they can run on their own and set hours that cater to their lifestyle. They do most of the work alone. But they may not really have a business; they could have a "glorified job." The real risk for them is that if they can't show up for work, they risk loosing it all!

There is also the small business owner who has structured their business to run and grow without having to be there all the time. This is true freedom; most people consider this financial freedom. It means you have a business that prospers and grows without constant hard work. It continues to generate income that flows easily to the owner.

Your success in growing a business also depends on the amount of personal freedom you want. And your degree of freedom is determined by your willingness to delegate to others so the company can grow without you having to run day-to-day operations.

Planning Your Way to Growth

Whether you consider yourself a business owner, an entrepreneur, or a little of both, the key is to envision, plan, and articulate what you see in the future for yourself and your team. If you can't articulate a growth plan, you don't own it. Owning your business growth plan means writing it down and discussing it in detail with everyone involved.

The problem is that most business owners and entrepreneurs have no plan at all. That's nonsense! Nothing committed to paper, nothing planned for growth. Any plan is better than no plan at all!

A business plan requires a well-thought-out plan for growth. However, you don't need a two-inch binder full of complicated documents. Often, a one-page business plan can be more powerful than a traditional plan because it's easier to implement.

Writing a one-page business plan is also a helpful exercise because it requires you to think critically about the business. It forces you to make a plan and get right to the point. It can be very eye-opening because it shows you exactly where you need to focus to gain the best results for growth.

A business plan also allows you to measure success and keep score. You must condense your thoughts and explain yourself clearly so prospective investors can quickly understand your business. Let's take a quick look (an executive summary, if you will) at what constitutes a simple business plan.

Elements of a Traditional Business Plan

A traditional business plan includes:

- A summary of the business concept, including key success factors
- A vision statement and success milestones
- A market analysis, including target market and customer characteristics
- The nature of your competition, including opportunities for strategic growth
- Products and services description and positioning
- A sales and marketing plan for advertising and promotion
- A list of key personnel or customer service support
- Profit & loss (P&L) projections, including cash flow and expense sheet

A one-page business plan follows the same basic structure, but with certain aspects either shortened or omitted. It includes the business concept, current business situation, key success factors, and financials.

A business plan isn't busywork. It's a clear and concise way to move into action that forces you to think critically about your business. A business plan can serve many other purposes. For example, if you are writing a plan to secure investors, emphasize the areas that will impress them the most.

In a simple business plan, focus on one or two areas. Your plan must be a well-written, clearly defined document that describes the nature of your business. This should include your sales and marketing strategy, the business's financial background, and a projected P&L statement.

MY BUSINESS PLAN LED TO A SUCCESSFUL BUSINESS SALE

When I owned my retail clothing stores, I put together a business plan that focused on the overall business value. It included details of my business income, marketing plan, record growth, and profits. The goal was to have something I could show to a prospective buyer, even though I was not planning on selling the business for another year or two.

Within 30 days of writing out the business plan, one of my loyal customers came into the store and said, "I want you to hear it from me first. I'm looking into opening a clothing store in the new shopping center next door."

Knowing she had no retail or business experience whatsoever and would have a hard time competing with me, I asked, "Why would you want to compete with me when I have most of the best clothing lines tied up and a successful business already?" What I said next rolled out so naturally: "Why don't you just buy my business?"

Shocked, she responded, "I had no idea it was for sale!"

Well, as of that day, my business *was* for sale, since I had found the perfect buyer. We went into my office and looked at my new business plan, and within 30 days, I had sold my business for full asking price.

Keep in mind that your business plan should change as your business does. Therefore, revise your business plan each new year. Write out goals for three or four areas to focus on for the year so you can drive revenues, deliver value for your customers, improve profitability, or otherwise grow your business.

Your business plan serves as a road map so your business can plan its future and you can avoid bumps in the road. This is especially important to keep in mind if you're self-funding or bootstrapping your business. When you define your plan, make sure you also plan for your future success. This may eventually include expanding or selling the business.

A business plan can also provide a Plan B, so consider this when putting the plan together. In my case, my Plan B was part of my original Plan A—my plan to "build to sell."

The Five Defining Stages of Business Growth

Many companies start out as a simple idea. If a business reaches its full potential, it has passed through five very distinct stages. These five stages are based on critical points, which a business owner or entrepreneur must handle to remain on a growth path. If they fail to meet these challenges, they will face a decline in profits.

As a rule, if a business is growing according to plan, each of these stages lasts about three years, although you can cut down on that time by doing more planning and strategic thinking. An exception is the business concept stage, which usually takes about six to nine months.

A business must grow and pass through these different stages of development or die in the attempt. Therefore, the end of each of these five stages marks a dangerous period in which the business must break through to reach the next level. Let's walk through each of them.

Stage 1: The Business Concept

This is one of the most exciting times in a business venture. At this early level, the owner or entrepreneur is motivated and optimistic. Coming up with ideas for products and services to sell, nurturing those ideas into a reality, and then turning that reality into a viable, ongoing business is the most enjoyable experience for any entrepreneur. But once the business plan is written and the owner is fully committed to making the business profitable, it is time to get into action and move the business to the second stage.

Stage 2: The Established Business

The business is up and running and beginning to establish a name for itself. The owner is focused on obtaining customers, increasing sales, and improving marketing efforts. The owner is active in the business, performing most or all of the important tasks, and is the major source of energy and direction that keeps the business moving forward. There are many businesses that don't move on to the next stage, even after being in business for many years. Once the owner commits to becoming more organized and learns how to overcome obstacles, the business is positioned for the next stage.

Stage 3: The Systems Startup

When a business reaches this stage, it is experiencing a more disciplined and programmed way of doing business. It should have a solid sales and marketing plan in place. The systems stage requires a high degree of control over the entire operation. The owner may still be hands-on, but she should start focusing more on the business than on day-to-day operations. She is probably dealing with staff responsibilities and recognizing the need for training. At this point, there is likely no strategy in place to maximize the training programs needed to ensure continued customer service success. It is critical to put in place consistent sales and service strategies at this time. Systems give the business the support it needs for smooth operation.

Stage 4: "Success Is Easy"

At this stage, success flows easily. The business owner is more focused on results than on daily efforts. There is a strong vision for where the company is headed. The owner learns how to delegate and builds a supportive team to help grow the business. The plan is to keep the company stable and profitable for long-term success. To achieve this, the owner must use his increased freedom to pursue a new startup division or find another income stream for the business.

Stage 5: The Next Strategy

At this stage, the business and the owner have matured and reached a level of financial freedom.

As the business continues to grow, it may need to reinvent itself as the industry and market change around it. This may require a new brand strategy and customer focus. If a dramatic reinvention is required, the five-stage cycle begins all over again, and the business will then redevelop and move through the cycle to achieve maximum success.

Develop Systems for Consistent Growth

It's critical to put systems into your business. Systems are designed to connect all the daily business functions and action steps together to create an easy and effortless flow. A system connects the puzzle pieces of a business together to allow you to implement a consistent business strategy.

Creating systems is one way to avoid ongoing obstacles and challenges and a great way to grow a successful company. Systems also require business owners and entrepreneurs to delegate effectively so they can work on expanding the business and increasing their professional skills.

After reading the book *The E-Myth Revisited* by Michael Gerber, I had a new way of looking at my business. From that day forward, I started adding systems into my business in everything, including hiring, inventory, marketing, following up with customers, etc. Not only did those systems pay off in day-to-day operations, but they also paid off when I added a new location and when I sold my company.

Without smart systems in place, your business won't grow to the levels you want. Systems serve as your company's essential building blocks, make your processes run predictably, and make change easier to accomplish. When change impacts your business, knowing what systems need to be modified becomes even easier.

Creating systems in your business also creates a tremendous amount of value. For example, if you are selling your business or a business concept franchise, formal procedures really add up. A buyer can quickly see that your operations run smoothly and consistently, which is critically important when it comes to attracting investors.

Systems really came into play with the franchise phenomenon. One of the first franchises developed was McDonald's, which ranks at the top of the global franchise list today. In 1954, Ray Kroc, a traveling milkshake machine salesman, discovered a hamburger stand in San Bernardino, California, that was owned by the two McDonald brothers. Ray had not seen anything like the system these brothers had created. A limited menu of burgers, fries, and drinks were made quickly and inexpensively. He was amazed at how the business ran like clockwork. He had a vision the McDonald brothers could not see: a duplicatable, moneymaking machine.

Ray Kroc persuaded the two brothers to franchise the system and later bought them out, going on to create the largest franchise system in the world today. McDonald's success is truly amazing! It has grown into a network of more than 35,000 locations in more than 100 countries.

The model continues to grow, proving that systems work and can help a company achieve sustainable growth—no matter what kind of business you own.

Shameless, No-Nonsense Action Steps and Affirmation

Success Is Easy Affirmation (say it, believe it, and own it): "Success comes easy to me because I have a structured system for my business that keeps growth and success consistent."

> 1. *Find someone to guide you to make success easier.* Connect with a mentor or consultant who can expand your vision for growth.

Remain coachable, open, and willing to ask for help. Engage in some form of accountability to ensure your success. Success is easy with accountability partners, mentors, or mastermind groups. A business consultant may provide an effective level of accountability. Someone smarter and more successful than yourself can help you with critical thinking and strategic planning to help determine a direction for your continued growth. When you are held accountable, you are forced to expand and grow. When you are guided, you fast track your success!

2. *Plan, envision, and articulate what you see in the future for yourself and your team.* Write down and discuss your business growth plan in detail with everyone on your team. Learn how to delegate and create more freedom and time. Your personal freedom is determined by your willingness to delegate to others so that your business can grow without your presence in day-to-day operations.

3. *Recognize the various stages of business growth.* Knowing what phase you are in will help you assess your current success while making plans for the future that you can execute with ease. A business must pass through five different stages of development to achieve maximum growth.

4. *Create a simple business plan.* It should include the overall business concept, current business situation, key success factors, and financials. Your business plan serves as a road map so you can plan for the future and avoid bumps in the road. This is especially important if you're self-funding or bootstrapping a business.

5. *Develop systems for growth.* Systems are designed to connect all the daily functions and action steps to create an easy and effortless flow. A system connects the puzzle pieces of a business together to allow it to run smoothly and consistently. By adding systems to your business, you create a tremendous amount of value in the eyes of a buyer or investor.

SUCCESS IS EASY . . .
with Change and Reinvention

One thing holding most people back from success (besides their mindset) is resistance to change. Change requires you to do something outside your limitation zone. You may need to ask for money or help. You may need to raise prices, make cold calls, or anything outside of your limitation zone.

The key to accepting change is to first understand why you're resisting. Let's face it—change can be challenging and scary. But everything must change. If you don't change and/or reinvent your business at times, it will stop growing.

In this chapter, you will discover the biggest obstacles to change and how to overcome them. You will also learn that change can be forced on you for good, because success itself brings on change.

Playing to Win Instead of Playing Not to Lose

You simply can't play it safe if you want to succeed! It's time to shift your focus to recognizing what you stand to lose if you don't change. When change happens, you should start playing to win instead of playing not to lose. There is a big difference.

Resistance to change defies the laws of nature. The earth, the universe, and life itself are in a perpetual state of change. The no-nonsense reality is that you can't ignore change!

Sometimes change requires reinvention, where you break new ground. Other times, it moves toward innovation, which helps you do old things in new ways. You can't do something new and creative from the same old rut. Doing the same thing every day is madness. There's no adventure in sameness, which destroys creativity, innovation, and fun.

Embrace the unknown, shake things up, and be willing to rock the boat and be shameless in your pursuit of change!

The only way you're ever going to know if a change is right is to experience it. If it's wrong, you'll find out in time, and then you can adjust. Business is a process of making constant adjustments and corrections. However, most people fear making a mistake so much that they are unwilling to change, which means they never even reach the finish line.

Start looking at change as a friend instead of an enemy. Allow it to work for you instead of against you. When you stop resisting change and look forward to a new and better experience, something good will happen. Good things come when you're ready to change!

There are circumstances in the world you can fairly label as hard. Change is not one of them. Learn not to fear challenges by sharpening your willpower. Use change as a bridge between where you are now and where you want to be.

The biggest obstacles to change are lack of motivation, lack of knowledge, and fear. You will not change if you don't know where the change is taking you. Decide the destination, and get shameless in your resolution to get there.

When you are determined to achieve your goals through change, it sets you well above the average person, who will continue to quit things on a regular basis. This bad habit will cause them to fail because they will be playing not to lose instead of playing to win.

Expand Your Level of Awareness to Change

Every decision and action you take in business and life is based on your level of awareness. At any given moment, if you want to be all you can be, you must work to change and expand your awareness. In other words, to make perception a reality, picture your desired outcome. Be acutely aware of what you need to change and how you need to make that change happen. Real growth and change start from the inside out by first changing the picture in your mind.

Although deciding to change is not hard, changing a habit and fulfilling your dreams requires work—but the process is fun. When you change and grow, an incredible feeling of self-empowerment, awareness, and joy comes to you.

Change Can Become a Force for Good

Plenty of successful people chose to make major career changes far into adulthood. For example, Julia Child worked in advertising from 1935 to 1942 and didn't launch her successful career as a celebrity chef until age 50.

Long before Ronald Reagan became the only Hollywood movie actor to become president of the United States, he switched careers from film and TV to become governor of California at age 56. Though very different people, both used the power of change to completely re-envision their lives.

Success requires you to redefine and reinvent what is most important to you. Often, change is forced on you for many reasons. You may feel the need for change because you've grown beyond your current business and feel bored or unchallenged by your daily routine. You may feel stuck or like you're missing out on something. You may want to run away from where you are and plunge into something new. Whatever you are feeling, change can force you to do something different.

Often you achieve a certain level of success and then want to switch to something new. When this happens, you don't need to change everything about yourself. Rather, you take all your knowledge, skills, and experience with you to the next chapter in your life.

As a business consultant, I have worked with dozens of clients who came to me for help in changing what they do. Many had an idea of what they wanted to do for a business but had limited or no knowledge of where to begin. Others were stuck, without the faintest idea of how to start. The only thing they knew is that they needed a change. Some were retired from a corporate job, while others had left long-term careers and didn't want another job. But neither group had any idea how to become an entrepreneur.

And there was a third group: business owners hoping to teach other people what they knew as a coach or consultant. For example, my client Glenn Michael Milliet wanted to leave his highly successful hair salon after 40 years. Glenn generated millions of dollars from his salon, was well-known, and was considered a star in the industry, but he wanted to make a dramatic change in his business and personal life.

He discovered that his success was due more to his ability to communicate with his clients than his ability to cut hair. Because of this talent for communicating, Glenn was asked to train the professional sales teams at Procter & Gamble and Paul Mitchell.

His training launched these companies to their highest sales records in decades. Glenn was then asked to speak at some of the largest industry trade shows across the U.S. Soon, he discovered that he enjoyed speaking and teaching more than working in the salon. He was ready for a dramatic change, but he didn't know how to take the next step.

"When the student is ready, the teacher will appear." We've heard this saying before. I believe it's true because when you are ready for change, your awareness is at an all-time high. I met Glenn while I was speaking in Louisiana, and he asked me to mentor him in building his new career as a professional speaker and business consultant.

Within a year, Glenn sold his Louisiana salon, moved to North Carolina to be near family, and completely changed his career. He's now a full-time professional speaker and consultant who hosts workshops throughout the U.S.—thanks to using change as his superpower.

Success Itself Fosters Change

Not only do you make changes to earn success, but success itself can also bring changes to your life and business. The greater the success, the greater the change.

This certainly was the case for me when I moved away from my partnership and my world speaking tour. Even if you have a successful business, that doesn't necessarily mean you have everything you want out of life. Imagine being highly successful right now.

- Would you live where you're living now?
- Would you do the same things and travel to the same places?
- Would you wear the same clothes and drive the same car?
- What portions of your personal life and freedom would change?

Heraclitus, an ancient Greek philosopher, once posited that the only thing that is constant is change. The concept comes up frequently in the business world and is a reminder that how you react to constant change can determine your success.

When you welcome change and find ways to turn the unexpected into an opportunity for growth, it makes success easy. Having the right attitude about change can mean the difference between failing to achieve your goals or dealing with the changes and growing because of them.

Change can give birth to your greatest life successes if you open yourself to the possibilities. It allows you to think outside yourself and dream of what's possible. Your dreams can become your reality if you allow yourself to make consistent change happen. True happiness comes from meeting life's changes and overcoming challenges while remaining true to yourself, knowing that you have lived your life to the fullest. But you have to want to change.

I've learned that nothing is permanent. Everything must change sooner or later. Some changes are small bumps in the road and others are big hills you have to climb over to get to the other side.

Change requires decisions—some small, some big—but making decisions, even if they're wrong, is better than sitting still and hoping things will work out. Deciding to change something already makes you successful.

Change has been forced on me so many times in my life and career that I've lost count. I've built and sold so many companies and reinvented myself so many times I could be crowned the Queen of Reinvention. Oh, yeah—that already happened. I own the tiara!

MAKING THE DECISION FOR A BIG CHANGE

Reinvention is kind of like Kenny Rogers' song "The Gambler." You have to know when to stop wasting energy and resources on a situation.

I hear this song in my head whenever I think about the time I walked away from a business partnership. I had to take a gamble and decide when to run. It was not an easy decision to make because I was making great money and traveling the world on an exciting speaking tour.

I learned a lot from working with my business partner. I enjoyed the travel, and I had the opportunity to speak in multiple countries. Our business was flourishing, but I didn't feel successful in my personal life. I needed to make a change.

MAKING THE DECISION FOR A BIG CHANGE, continued

As I pondered my decision, I started working more in the U.S. with less international travel. That gave me the chance to meet my husband, Greg. My personal life started to turn around, but my business partnership began to fall apart.

Maybe I hadn't realized how unbalanced the partnership was before my personal life improved. Or maybe I had simply decided to ignore it because the business, for the most part, was successful. But once the realization set in, it was very clear that I was due for a dramatic change. The partnership was unbalanced because I took on most of the promotion and marketing, plus I was doing the bulk of work with the clients.

My motivation began to fade, and so did my marketing efforts. Our business started to drop. My partner would have continued because she was still happy with the way things were going. But I was not. I had to talk to her about making a change. It was not going to be an easy conversation, but in my head I had it all figured out. My goal was to go back to building my independent businesses but still partner with her on some events. I also wanted to move away from the international touring and bring our events back into the U.S. It all made perfect sense to me until I talked to my partner.

During dinner the first night of the tour in Australia, I explained my proposal. In my mind it was a clear-cut plan with an open-ended opportunity to continue working together. I felt good about the conversation, but I wasn't sure how my partner felt since she didn't say much. We said good night and planned to meet for breakfast the next morning.

At 5:00 A.M., she pounded on my hotel room door. I woke from a sound sleep and let her into the room with all her luggage. She told me she had rebooked her flight to head back to the U.S. that day.

I was shocked. I had no idea what she was thinking. Obviously, she had taken my conversation about the change as a complete end to our business relationship and a real threat to her income and future. Fear must have immediately set in, and she was not sure what to do.

She was very upset, and I asked her to sit down and talk it through before leaving. "We've been business partners and friends for years, please don't end it like this!" I said. "Let's talk. And how about the speaking tour? We need to finish the tour!"

MAKING THE DECISION FOR A BIG CHANGE, continued

She replied, "You can finish the tour. I have to get home and figure out what I'm going to do with my business and life now!" Knowing her plan made no sense and that she was reacting out of emotion, I asked her again to sit down so we could work things out. After hours of talking it over, we agreed to continue the speaking tour in Australia.

We did a couple more speaking engagements together after returning to the states, but our partnership came to an end within a few months. We both couldn't make it work any longer.

Afterward, I reinvented my business and brand strategy. I can personally relate to going from Stage 5 in business to starting over at Stage 1 again in the growth process (see Chapter 14). My business reinvention was not a quick fix, but it was ultimately massively rewarding because I decided to change in a big way.

Change Overcomes Fear

Success often makes people risk-averse. The instinct is to hold on to the things you're good at, fearful that if you reinvent yourself you may not replicate your original achievement.

It can be scary to leave the comforts of the familiar for the untested road ahead. Entrepreneurs often worry they can't win in business multiple times. But keep in mind that if your knowledge, skills, and expertise were up to the task once, you have the tools to win again!

People often like the idea of change more than change itself. These people are self-proclaimed risk takers, but in reality they usually play it safe. Successful people don't flatter themselves with talk of daring intentions, but they do make hard, challenging decisions. Push back your fear of the unknown and move forward with bold action.

And, if it helps, look to a mentor who models that fearlessness to show you how. The person in my life who taught me the most about accepting change was my grandmother Bernadette. Her amazing lesson in accepting change was both courageous and inspiring.

When my grandmother was 85 years old, she was not the healthy, active person she once was. Arthritis, high blood pressure, and pain left her dependent on a walker and cane to get around. Pain pills and lots of sleep helped her cope.

It was frustrating when the doctors told her there was nothing more they could do to help. At that point, my grandmother was weak and depressed, but she decided to try one last doctor, who suggested she try water therapy.

"Oh, no!" she said. "I never go near water. I'm deathly afraid of it." And with her great sense of humor, she added, "The closest I ever came to water was a walk on the beach. And that made me so nervous I had to go inside and have a Scotch and water."

After a little more convincing from the doctor, she reluctantly decided to give it a try. She was willing to accept change, even though she was fearful.

As she sat on the steps of the swimming pool the first day, shaking and afraid, the therapist coaxed her to get in and walk across the pool with the help of her walker. She did, and went back the next day, and the next. Each time it got a little easier for her to walk.

My grandmother built confidence and stamina as she improved. In a short time, she no longer needed the help of her physical therapists and joined a local health club to take up water aerobics. Her instructor was a fit 90-year-old man who was retired from the military. He inspired her to continue exercising and get even better.

After less than a year, my grandmother was free of pain and lived a very active lifestyle without the use of a walker or cane. In fact, her last few years of life were some of her happiest and most fulfilling. She lived to be 93 years "young," and just three weeks before she passed away, she was teaching water aerobics herself at the retirement

Reinvention = the action or process through which something changes so much it appears entirely new. Make reinvention work for you!

community where she lived. Hopefully, my grandmother's story will inspire and motivate you to accept more positive changes into your life, too.

Harness Change to Reinvent Yourself

Is it time for a reinvention? Is there some unfulfilled or untapped potential locked away inside you screaming to get out? Maybe you can hear it but can't seem to bring it out of yourself. But you know there is more you want to achieve. Internally, you have an intense desire to change, but externally things are not yet clear. All you know is what you are doing is no longer good enough. If it's no longer working for you, it may be time to make some drastic changes—maybe even a total reinvention.

Reinvention means letting go of those things that are holding you back from moving forward. It means letting go of habits that don't serve you and responsibilities that keep you from living life to the fullest. It means getting rid of marketing and branding strategies that are no longer effective. It means being open to complete change.

You already have the intense desire to change inside you, but truly changing yourself requires a process of self-discovery. You must find your purpose in life, discover new ways of thinking and acting, realize what your true beliefs are, and live by those standards.

Self-discovery requires personal growth, which is often challenging if you tend to resist change. If you're willing to be vulnerable and admit you don't have it all figured out, you've already taken your first step toward self-discovery and reinvention. Incredible changes are on the horizon!

Shameless, No-Nonsense Action Steps and Affirmation

Success Is Easy Affirmation (say it, believe it, and own it): "Success comes easy to me because I accept change and I'm open to a complete reinvention when required."

1. *Accept change.* The earth, the universe, and life itself are in a perpetual state of change. The no-nonsense reality is that you can't ignore change! The only way to know if change is right for you is to experience it. Real growth and change come from the inside by first changing the picture in your mind. When you change and grow, an incredible feeling of self-empowerment and joy appears.

2. *Decide to change what is no longer working in your business and life.* Everything must change sooner or later. Some changes are small bumps in the road, and others are big hills you must climb over to get to the other side. Embrace the unknown, shake things up, and be willing to rock the boat and be shameless in your pursuit of change!

3. *Accept risk over fear.* If you've succeeded already with your knowledge and skills, you have the tools, skills, and experience you need to win again! Learn not to fear challenging things by sharpening your willpower. Use change as a bridge between where you are now and where you want to go.

4. *Uncover the process of self-discovery.* This will allow you to find your true purpose and discover new ways of thinking and acting. Self-discovery requires personal growth, which is easy when you become vulnerable enough to be open to change. Success requires you to redefine and reinvent what is most important to you. You may feel stuck or as though you're missing out on something. That in turn may make you feel as if you want to run away and plunge into something new. Whatever you are feeling, change can force you to do something different.

5. *Start to look at change as a friend instead of an enemy.* Allow it to work for you instead of against you. When you stop fearing and resisting change and look forward to a new and better experience, something good will happen. Good things come when you're ready to change.

CHAPTER 16

SUCCESS IS EASY . . .
with Good Decision-Making Skills

Your success is largely determined by the choices you make. So why aren't more people equipped with useful decision-making skills? There are only so many hours in a day, so make the most of your time by making good decisions!

Decision making is unavoidable. Not making a decision is itself a decision, just not a very good one! One of the biggest responsibilities you have as a business owner or entrepreneur is to make important decisions every single day. The decisions you make directly impact your future success.

To paraphrase Lewis Carroll from *Alice in Wonderland*, if you don't know where you're going, any road will get you there. Decision-makers don't waste time. They think objectively and clearly, then narrow the focus on the desired direction.

We are all confronted with decisions to make on a daily basis. Some are small and minor, while others are huge and potentially life changing. Some are simple and obvious; others are more difficult and painstaking.

In this chapter, you will learn how to improve your decision-making skills. You will also learn how to move forward when you feel stuck. Ready? Good—let's get unstuck and make some decisions that lead you to greater success.

Make Decisions Faster and Better

While speed is a critical factor in your decision making, it's quality that matters most. A slow, methodical, analytic method is not necessarily the best approach to decision making.

The perfect solution seldom exists, but that doesn't stop a lot of people from an endless and unrealistic pursuit of the perfect decision. It's important to be careful and lay out the alternatives, but obsessing over them is a different matter. Obsessing over a decision takes a heavy toll on your time and emotional energy.

Delaying an important decision just slows you down and makes you worry. The decision will still be there waiting for you in the end. Don't overcomplicate things! Take ownership of the decision. Instead of waiting for the moons, stars, and planets to align—move on!

One of the best ways to make faster decisions is the "Quick Step" approach. Imagine only having a few minutes to make an important decision. Quickly run through all the elements, including the problem, objectives, consequences, and risk tolerance. Next, compare those to the overall benefits and outcomes of taking action. Do this in a matter of minutes. Don't get hung up on the details or worry about getting it perfect. Just decide to decide!

It can help to write out a rough sketch of the elements on a piece of paper. Work through the pieces of the decision to see the possible outcomes more clearly. Once you have a rough outline, you can go back later to tie up any loose ends on specific points. It's often a pleasant surprise to discover that the Quick Step approach helps you make better decisions faster. Eventually it becomes a habit.

Work on speeding up the process for small decisions to free up time for the big-picture decisions that really matter. When you make good business decisions quickly, you have a significant advantage over those who take a lot of time making up their minds.

If you need a little extra time to make a complex decision, plan a short deadline. The brief delay will give you just enough time to make sure the decision feels right before implementing it an the action plan.

How to Get Unstuck

There will be times when you just can't decide. Sometimes you'll find yourself stuck, unable to find a solution or make any forward progress. You may not know where to begin because of an obstacle that's getting in your way. And other times, despite analyzing the decision, you still can't make up your mind.

When this happens, remember to remain focused on the facts. Don't allow emotions to get in the way! It is much easier to make a decision when emotions are left out of the equation. There's an old saying: "Don't make permanent decisions based on temporary emotions." Successful people recognize when their emotions come into play and can weigh decisions as objectively and rationally as possible.

Keep in mind that every decision you make goes back to focusing on your vision and goals. Every time you make a tough choice, consider the choice that supports the vision. Below are five tips for better decision making:

1. *Find a solution to a decision-making problem by asking a successful person you trust.* Once you share and brainstorm the information, you can make connections you never saw before. Select your advisors wisely to help you make decisions beyond your experience level.

2. *Stop the perfectionism cycle.* Instead of seeking impossible perfection, you'll often need to take the leap first without having all the answers. Then simply trust that you're on the right path.

3. *Don't overthink it.* Learn to turn your overactive mind off for a while. Often your insight can come when you least expect it. By keeping your thoughts quiet, you may switch to a new thought process that will result in a different outcome.

4. *Admit it when you make a mistake.* If your decisions steer you wrong, fess up, correct the error, and move on. Even making the wrong decision will help you learn something. And when you admit to yourself and others that you were wrong, you gain respect for being humble, honest, and real.

5. *Don't try to solve a problem—simply decide.* The decision can *help* solve a problem, but not every problem can be solved by making a decision. Instead, decision making often relies more on intuition than over analysis. The solution often comes from your gut reaction, or what *feels* like the right decision.

Don't Take Advice from Chronic Advice Givers

Some people show more interest in solving your problems than their owns. Chronic advice givers often make outrageous and unsolicited suggestions, but just because they want to give you advice doesn't mean you have to listen to them.

Chronic advice givers are probably not going to help you make a logical decision anyway. They are usually too entrenched in the ego-gratifying habit of telling others what to do.

You know who these people are. You've probably got one or two in your friend and family circles. They're anxious people who like to claim they know something you don't and provide suggestions that are unfounded and often premature.

Do not accept advice from someone who is unqualified to dispense it. Why take success advice from someone who's unsuccessful?

Sometimes You Just Have to Trust Your Intuition

Psychologists define intuition as "a process that gives us the ability to know something directly without analytic reasoning, bridging the gap between the conscious and non-conscious parts of our mind, and also between instinct and reason. It is an automatic, effortless feeling that often motivates you to take action on a decision. Intuition involves trusting the sum total of your subconscious experiences. It draws on everything you've experienced for all the years you've been alive, which means it's constantly growing and evolving, just like you are" (https://www.psychologytoday.com/us/blog/the-intuitive-compass).

Some scientists have started calling your gut instincts or intuition the "second brain." Like your conscious mind, your gut absorbs and responds to information. You know what it feels like to have a hollow pit in your stomach as you weigh a decision. That's your gut talking to you loud and clear. But can it really compare to your conscious mind? Yes! Your gut or intuition doesn't just compare to the mind—it rivals it!

Intuition is also the result of a lot of processing that happens in the brain. Research suggests that the brain is a large, predictive machine, constantly comparing incoming sensory information and current experiences against your stored knowledge and memories of previous experiences to predict what will come next.

Trusting my intuition has paid off multiple times in business. In fact, I can't recall when my intuition didn't serve me well. For example, as a professional speaker I use intuition to "read" an audience before and during a presentation. This allows me to custom tailor my points so I can resonate with each audience differently. As a business consultant, I work individually with my clients to help each one build a strategic action plan. To do this, I must tap into my intuition, fed by my knowledge and years of experience, to help me quickly and confidently gain the source material and direction I need to support each client.

You may be surprised to learn intuition is a deliberate skill you can learn to develop. Simply start by paying more attention to it.

Once honed, it can apply in many situations, from helping you choose a career path to developing an action plan or making quick decisions under pressure.

When you have a question to answer or a decision to make, rely on your intuition. You might sell yourself short with limiting thoughts, but your intuition will never let you down. Learn to tap into it and trust it more!

Shameless, No-Nonsense Action Steps and Affirmation

Success Is Easy Affirmation (say it, believe it, and own it): "Success comes easy to me because I have good decision-making skills."

1. *Learn how to make faster and more productive decisions.* The perfect solution seldom exists, but that doesn't stop a lot of people from an endless, unrealistic pursuit of the perfect decision. It's important to be careful and lay out the alternatives, but obsessing over a decision takes a heavy toll on your time and emotional energy. Delaying an important decision slows you down and may cause you to worry. The decision will still be there waiting for you in the end, so don't overcomplicate things! Take ownership of it.

2. *Run through the elements of a decision to improve your decision-making skills.* These elements include the problem, objectives, consequences, and risk tolerance. Work on speeding up the process for small decisions to free up time for the big-picture decisions that really matter. Then implement the idea for a win!

3. *Focus on the facts.* Don't allow emotions to get in the way when it comes to business decisions. It's much easier to decide when emotions are left out of the equation. There's an old saying: "Don't make permanent decisions based on temporary emotions." Successful people look at decisions as objectively and rationally as possible. Learn how to put all emotions aside and make common-sense decisions quickly.

4. *Don't listen to chronic advice givers.* Just because they may want to give you advice doesn't mean you have to listen. Chronic advice givers are probably not going to help you make logical decisions anyway. Never accept advice from someone who is not qualified to dispense it. Select your advisors wisely to help you make decisions beyond your experience level.

5. *Trust your intuition when making a decision.* Intuition involves trusting the collection of your subconscious experiences. It draws on everything you've experienced for all the years you've been alive, which means it's constantly growing and evolving, just like you are. Anyone can learn to develop the power of their intuition. Simply start paying more attention to it. Once this skill is honed, it will help you make quick decisions under pressure.

SUCCESS IS EASY ...
with Persistence and Commitment

I magine for a moment that you have the power and persistence to achieve more success than you ever imagined, despite any obstacle placed in front of you.

It's easy to desire, dream, and imagine, but persistence requires you to move beyond when roadblocks are placed in front of you. You already have this power inside you—the power to never give up on yourself. Because what is waiting on the other side is too big to let go of.

Persistence is one of the top characteristics required to achieve your current and long-term goals. Persistence is more powerful than any other attribute you can possess. There is only one real difference between successful people who achieve their goals and unsuccessful people who struggle: Successful people are committed to overcoming all obstacles.

Persistence is so powerful it can make up for a lack of intelligence, knowledge, education, or experience. It can overcome almost any kind of adversity. Persistence is nothing more than continuous action in the face of massive rejection, frustration, and disappointment.

In this chapter, you will learn the importance of persistence and commitment when it comes to making success easy. You often hear these two words when describing someone else's success. Well, as long as you persist and stay committed in the right direction, making the right decisions, you will eventually find success.

You are about to learn how to regain power over obstacles and thrive during the most challenging times—like all successful people do.

To remain persistent and focused on what you want out of life, you must learn to become a strong self-motivator. No one will do it for you. You have to make it happen!

FROM A CARDBOARD HOUSE TO THE WHITE HOUSE

Turning dreams into persistence paid off in a huge way for motivational speaker Mona Dixon, who went from being homeless, sleeping on the streets and in shelters at the age of 13, to being honored in the Oval Office by President Obama when she was 17.

I met Mona at my Entrepreneurs of Phoenix MeetUp seminar in 2018. At the time she was a 24-year-old college student with big dreams. At first I was surprised she was so determined

FROM A CARDBOARD HOUSE TO THE WHITE HOUSE, continued

to become an entrepreneur at that age with no one to guide her on that path. She told me a little about her personal journey: homelessness, moving beyond it, and earning more than $100,000 in academic and achievement scholarships.

I invited her to a weekend event I was hosting the following month for entrepreneurs. She attended and soaked up every bit of information I shared. Before the weekend was over, she came up to me and said, "I want you to be my personal mentor. I'm going to find a way to invest in the program."

How does a broke college student find more than $20,000 to invest in a business mentor? She was persistent and committed to finding a way to make it happen, like she had been for every other goal in her life. So she found an investor.

Working with Mona was an honor and a thrill for me. She continues to inspire others as a motivational speaker and teen empowerment coach, sharing her story of walking into the Boys & Girls Clubs of America and discovering a life-changing opportunity. That day, new doors opened for her and changed her life forever. Soon after, she received a coveted National Youth of the Year Award from the organization, and she was invited and paid to speak by various Boys & Girls Clubs.

Mona now gives talks across the nation at Boys & Girls Clubs, schools, corporate philanthropic events, nonprofit fundraisers, and homeless shelters, seeking to motivate and inspire others to have a greater impact on their lives and their communities, despite any adversity they face. In 2015, President Obama appointed her as the youngest member of the Corporation for National and Community Service, which seeks to increase civic participation through volunteering and service.

Mona's commitment to excellence has allowed her to achieve more than she ever imagined. And she's only just beginning. She started her own nonprofit, the Inspired by Mona Foundation, to provide teens with opportunities, resources, and real-life skills for success. She is the picture of persistence.

Regain Power Over Obstacles

Obstacles are always present in everyday life, whether they set you back, stall your progress, or derail your best-laid plans for success. Obstacles are discouraging, especially when you are moving full speed ahead on your goals. Yet it's important to look beyond the barrier and see what purpose or lesson it serves so you can persist in your pursuit of success.

Could there be a greater lesson contained in the obstacle that you need to learn? Was the obstacle placed there to slow you down so you would pay attention? Perhaps you need to gain a new skill or some valuable knowledge before proceeding with your plans.

Obstacles often serve a role other than causing you emotional distress. In reality, obstacles can help in many ways because they can make you stronger.

Learning to overcome your challenges helps you move through an obstacle rather than allow it to dominate your life and stop you in your tracks. This enables you to embrace life without hesitation. When you stop letting obstacles bring you to a standstill, you start to look at them as a lesson rather than an impediment, and you can begin to identify their significance.

However, you must be willing to redirect your efforts when multiple attempts are getting you nowhere. The following five shameless, no-nonsense strategies will help you reclaim your power over obstacles when they appear in your way.

Strategy 1: Seek Out Helpful Advice

You may lack the knowledge or the abilities to overcome the obstacle on your own. Consider asking for help from others who support your success. Talk to friends or business associates who can look at the obstacle from another viewpoint. You are often too close to your own challenges to see beyond the obstacles by yourself.

Strategy 2: Don't Allow Emotions to Get in the Way

When faced with an obstacle, your emotions can run high because you get caught in crisis mode. This can cause you to overreact and create chaos. Yet when you step back from how the situation makes you feel, you'll see things with a clearer perspective and approach the obstacle with more common sense. Using sound judgment helps avoid an emotional reaction to the obstacle.

Strategy 3: Gain a New Perspective

Gaining new insight helps you step away from the chaos and fear. A new perspective helps you look at the obstacle from different vantage points while considering your options. Evaluating the obstacle in this way helps you see it differently and allows you to build on your personal power.

Strategy 4: Stay Committed and Persistent to Achieve Your Goals

Obstacles are not placed in front of you to weaken you. They are personal invitations to do more than the average person so you can succeed! Obstacles help you find true power as you achieve clarity on your process. When you remain persistent, obstacles assist you in finding a new way of reaching your goals.

For example, Thomas Edison's teacher called him "addled," and his mother ended up taking him out of school and teaching him at home. He was fired from his first two jobs for being "nonproductive." Later, Edison made 1,000 unsuccessful attempts at inventing the light bulb. He was committed to achieving his goal despite an endless stream of obstacles. Yet, today we don't remember his failures. We only remember his amazing successes!

Strategy 5: Develop a New Mindset Around Obstacles

When you allow your old thinking to disappear, new ways of thinking arrive—and obstacles fade away. Don't allow setbacks to weaken your mind. You are bound to encounter many setbacks in business and in life. Obstacles help enrich your mental experience and personal growth. They help you build resilience, commitment, strength, and self-confidence. Every time you tackle another obstacle, you overcome a mental hurdle and become more powerful.

The persistence and commitment to stick with your vision and goals, despite the odds, is key to reaching your limitless success potential. When you have a no-quit attitude and an unstoppable mindset, you will be able to persevere, succeed, and thrive during even the most challenging times.

THRIVING DURING MY MOST CHALLENGING TIME

In 2008, the real estate bubble in the U.S. housing market crashed and the economy began to plummet, and so did my professional speaking career. At the time, I was speaking mostly in the retail, mortgage, and real estate industries. My speaking opportunities fell off dramatically, and my income dropped practically overnight. Overall, meetings in the U.S. were drastically cut, and opportunities for paid professional speakers dried up. It was not looking good for my speaking career or my other business ventures.

I was having a hard time filling the seats at my event company, since people had less money to travel and invest in business. I also owned a real estate business, where we invested in residential fix-and-flip houses. Those investments took a deep dive.

The U.S. economy was in serious trouble, and almost everyone was feeling the financial pressure, including me. This was the most challenging obstacle I've ever experienced, and there was no quick fix to turn things around. It would take years to repair the economy, and it would get worse before it got better.

At first, I allowed my emotions to get the better of me. I couldn't see beyond this huge obstacle. It seemed too big to overcome. So I reached out to my brother, Terry, who had also been an entrepreneur all his adult life. I said, "Things are so bad that every one of my businesses has taken a hit, and for the first time, I can't figure out how to turn things around. I need your help to brainstorm some ideas with me."

Terry was just as concerned about his business as I was about mine. We talked for a long time, supporting each other with ideas and talking about our biggest fear: having to get a job! That fear gave us the motivation we needed to find a way around our obstacles.

THRIVING DURING MY MOST CHALLENGING TIME, continued

Sharing ideas and getting motivated again helped me kick into high gear. Luckily, we both have strong business skills, and we figured out creative ways to take action and gain momentum again.

It was time to change things up if I was going to survive this crisis. I had years of experience and expertise as a professional speaker, so I knew I could get work if I could find the opportunities. That's when the lightning bolt came to me. I realized there's a big world out there, and if I moved my marketing efforts outside the U.S., more people around the world could hire me and be inspired by my message.

Within three months of shifting my marketing efforts, many new opportunities began to appear, and soon 80 percent of my speaking business was overseas. I actually found it easy to get speaking opportunities outside of the U.S. due to the skills I had developed in my professional speaking business.

During my international travels, I started attending some of the multi-speaker "pitch fest" type of events that were popular around that time. These events featured about a dozen speakers over a three-day event, each one having 60 to 90 minutes on stage. Each speaker made an offer with their programs at the end of their talk, many of them were internet marketing programs back then.

I sat in amazement as droves of audience members ran to the back of the room after each speaker and bought their programs. And what shocked me the most was that most of them where actually "bad" speakers—but they where obviously good salespeople. It didn't matter, people wanted to buy hope. They wanted the "magic pill," the latest internet marketing system that would make them successful and maybe even rich.

And I sat there thinking—what am I missing here! I've worked so hard for so many years honing my craft as a professional speaker to be good enough to get paid well, and yet these "bad" speakers are killing it by walking away with a hell of a lot more money than I am as a paid professional speaker.

THRIVING DURING MY MOST CHALLENGING TIME, continued

Ding-ding! OK, I got it! They learned a different skill. They learned how to "sell" from stage, and they just happen to use speaking to deliver their offer.

A brand new opportunity had been placed in front of me—I just had to pay attention. And trust me when I say, I would not have paid attention if the economy didn't force me to. But now I'm glad it did force me to learn a new skill so that I can says "yes" or "no" to any speaking engagement that best fits my goals.

Next, it became my new goal to learn this skill of speaking and selling onstage. In fact, I now teach it to students myself and call it "Educate to Sell." Learning to sell with the delivery through speaking has opened up many new and exciting ways for me and my clients to have more success and to make more money. Anyone who considers themselves an expert at something and has a product, system or service to sell can make an authentic offer without having to be a professional speaker.

This new discovery was a huge blessing in disguise for my speaking business. And it came about at the perfect time, when the economy had taken a huge downturn for paid professional speakers.

This was a completely different way of doing business for me, which was a challenging mindset shift at first. I was going from being one of the highest paid professional speakers to having to speak for free in return for hoping to make a sale as I learned this new skill. Back then I was waiving my speaking fee, paying for all my own travel expenses, and taking on all the risk, all in hopes that I might sell enough to pay my expenses and turn a profit. It sounded crazy at first. Yet, this economic obstacle gave me a new survival tool that gained me ten times more than my typical speaking fee once I mastered this new skill of selling from the stage.

Lesson Learned: Get off your "high horse" to ride a new horse. Be willing to set your ego aside and learn a new way of doing business when times get challenging. Pay attention to what's going on around you and adapt with new skills. And when you learn how to use those new skills successfully, you can look back and say, "Damn, I can't believe I did that!"

Life often hands you obstacles so you are forced to invent a better way of doing things.

Shameless, No-Nonsense Action Steps and Affirmation

Success Is Easy Affirmation (say it, believe it, and own it): "Success comes easy to me because I have the persistence and commitment to achieve my goals no matter what gets in my way."

1. *Look beyond obstacles and discover what purpose or lesson they serve.* This will help you regain power over the obstacle in front of you. Perhaps you need to gain a new skill or some valuable knowledge before proceeding with your plan. The persistence and commitment to stick with your vision and goals, despite the odds, is key to reaching your limitless success potential. When you have a no-quit attitude and an unstoppable mindset, you can succeed and thrive during even the most challenging times.

2. *Don't allow emotions to get in the way of good common business sense.* When you step back from your emotions, you'll see things from a clearer perspective and approach the obstacle with sound judgment. Life often hands us obstacles so that we are forced to reinvent a better way of doing things.

3. *Gain a new perspective.* A new perspective helps you look at the obstacle from different vantage points while considering other options. One way to gain a new perspective is to increase your awareness. One of the most important things in life is to be aware of yourself and what's going on around you in the moment.

4. *Stay committed and persistent to achieving your goals.* Obstacles are placed in front of you as personal invitations to

do more than the average person to succeed! I strongly believe everything happens for a reason. You may not know why an obstacle is placed in front of you at the time, but if you pay attention, the lessons will appear.

5. *Develop a new mindset around obstacles.* Don't allow setbacks to weaken your mind. The persistence and commitment to stick with your vision and goals, despite the odds, is key to keep pushing toward your unlimited success potential. How you react to obstacles and challenges defines your level of success! Decide to play big despite the odds! Something magical happens the moment we decide to play all out to win in business and in life!

stepping up
to a higher level
of success

SUCCESS IS EASY . . .
as a Lifelong Learner

I f you were to survey highly successful people, you
would discover they share a philosophy of being
lifelong learners. Successful people always continue
to learn and grow. Unsuccessful people think, "I already
know enough to get by."

It's probably been a while since you left school, where
you probably felt forced to learn. Since then, you may
have lost the habit of learning new things or might not
have remained motivated enough to continue to expand
your knowledge.

Getting a formal education is not enough to sustain your success. What you learned in school may have given you an understanding of the fundamentals. However, most of what you learned comes down to memory and recall. While schools can provide you with a solid specialized education, lifelong learning provides you with a life education. This helps you live at a higher level of awareness so you can have everything you desire in every area of your life.

Making the commitment to lifelong learning isn't easy. Most people have a negative view of continuing education, but this works to your advantage. What others can't commit to is your opportunity. Every day when you commit to learning, growing, and developing yourself, it adds value to who you are and what you have to offer. As you increase your value, you also gain the rewards and compensation of knowledge, skills, and income.

To thrive and win in business, you must set higher standards for yourself by shifting your perspective on what learning means. The world is changing around you every day, so you must continue to learn to stay ahead of the game.

When you dedicate yourself to lifelong learning, you commit to improving each day, in every area of life. This includes your level of success, finances, health, and soft skills. These skills help you connect with others and with the world around you, not just in business but in your personal relationships, too.

In this chapter, you will discover that becoming a lifelong learner is a must if you want to achieve and maintain success in our ever-changing world.

Commit to Expanding Your Areas of Expertise

To be a successful lifelong learner, make a commitment early to expand your horizons by making room for new topics of inspiration in your life. Easy ways to start moving toward success are by reading empowering books and finding inspiring people to learn from on a daily basis.

Commit to learning things that are relevant to your industry and business, and commit to sharpening timeless, applicable skills that will help you move forward every day.

Expanding your knowledge comes down to diving deeper into your areas of expertise. Learning at this level puts you in a positive state of mind and inspires you to raise your standards and increase your value as an expert. Basically this is a process of positioning yourself as an expert. Improving yourself at this level takes dedication, discipline, and focus that the average person finds daunting, and it moves you light-years ahead of your competition.

Improve Your Quality of Life Through Learning

The more you learn, the more you realize there are exciting goals ahead of you. I learned this later in life. I was a poor student in school who hated to read and study. In fact, my high school English teacher came down on me hard at one point and told me that if I didn't pass the next test, I would be lucky to graduate. I would like to see that teacher again today and tell her I've now written nine books, many of them bestsellers.

Things changed dramatically after high school, when I had a chance to study what I wanted to learn: anything that could help me become successful.

As you continue to learn, you also learn more about yourself and create a greater quality of life: increased earning power, more opportunities, and amazing experiences. When you commit to lifelong learning, you are creating a need to constantly improve yourself so you can gain a competitive edge in business.

Your ultimate goal should be to live a life where you see no boundaries, because with your extended knowledge, you have the options to create anything you desire.

Growing up in a small town in Indiana, I had no idea I would one day travel all over the world, embrace new cultures, and learn more from the experiences that any book could ever teach me. Most of the people in my hometown have stayed the same since high school. Many have never traveled outside the U.S. and stopped learning and growing a long time ago. But I was able to break the mold and move away. I gained one of the most priceless gifts of all: worldly wisdom. I feel very blessed and deeply grateful for this gift. So remember that you can't allow others to put limitations on you. You must break free and achieve much more success than others expect of you!

The Lifelong Learner Mindset

To commit to being a lifelong learner, you must cultivate the right mindset. A lifelong learning mindset requires curiosity about the world. A curious mind wants to know more. It longs for new challenges, ideas, and experiences. It's not satisfied with the status quo. When you have this mindset, you want to grow, learn, and develop beyond imagination. You want to become a well-rounded, better version of yourself.

The lifelong learner mindset is always open to new possibilities, and you come to understand that the only way to reach your ultimate success potential is to be open to anything that comes your way and be willing to explore everything.

This mindset also allows you to approach life from a place of gratitude, where nothing is taken for granted. Every bit of knowledge you've learned is appreciated and respected because you understand that over time it will help transform your perspective on life.

This process of lifelong learning isn't just about reading lots of books to gather information, although I have read hundreds of books. It's also about taking the information you acquire and putting it into practice.

Implementing the Lessons Life Teaches You

We all have weaknesses in our personal lives that we can improve on. Our personal life has a tendency to spill out onto the rest of our life, including our business relationships. That's why it's important to become a lifelong learner in your personal development, too. I'm not saying you should become a personal development junkie who attends event after event in search of enlightenment. Self-awareness and enlightenment are great, but you have to implement what you learn in your life or it's worthless!

I've had to work through weak areas of my personal life and implement the lessons I learned along the way. In fact, it never stops. I continue to work on my personal development and growth to this day. My personal-development journey started decades ago when I started reading books that inspired me with new insights and self-awareness.

Some of my favorite books at the time included *The Four Agreements* by Don Miguel Ruiz, *The New Psycho-Cybernetics* by Maxwell Maltz, and *Real Moments* by Barbara De Angelis, Ph.D. As I read, I felt as if each book was written especially for me at that time in my life.

After reading many personal-development books, I also attending a few personal development events. Some of these events can be very helpful to move you past limitation zones when they are taught by ethical and profoundly wise teachers such as personal-development mentor, Barbara De Angelis. Barbara helped change my life in many ways, not just personally. At the time, I had been speaking professionally about business for about eight years. Barbara told me something was missing from my speaking skill set. She said, "You haven't gone deep enough yet! You haven't reached the level that will allow you to tap into your ultimate potential. You have much more to give. You must learn how to tap into both your head and your heart when you speak."

I replied, "No, my business is fine. I'm doing great and making lots of money. After all, I'm teaching business. How is tapping into my heart going to make a difference in the business world?"

Barbara said, "You don't get it yet. You're missing out on the deep connections you can have with yourself and your audience. When I teach you how to connect both your head and heart, you will feel the shift."

I practiced Barbara's advice as I went back out to speak. Each time, I tapped into my head and my heart a little more, as she had taught me. When I finally tapped in all the way, it did allow a complete and authentic connection with the audience. This personal transformation was profound, and it has given me a new skill I can use for the rest of my life, both from stage and with my consulting clients.

Shared Thinking Can Expand Your Mindset

When you want to learn a new skill, do you go off by yourself and try to figure it out, or do you find someone to show you how so you learn faster? Shared thinking returns greater value than solo thinking because when you learn from others, it's much easier than trying to work things out on your own—and it yields a higher return on your investment of time.

The compounding action of shared thinking with successful people moves your knowledge forward faster and easier. I've discovered that the more I respect the wisdom of others, the more I listen and learn. For example, when I'm being mentored by someone, I allow that person to do most of the talking so I can learn from them. When I'm mentoring a client, on the other hand, I ask them a few questions and expect to do most of the talking, so the client can learn from me. In shared business relationships, it's more of a give-and-take conversation between equals.

Even beyond the immediate need to solve a particular problem, listening to how others approach business or their personal lives can flip a switch in your thinking, leading to a breakthrough or a new insight. When you're excited to learn more, you do more, and work becomes more like play!

You could lose everything you have now, and you still wouldn't lose the knowledge, wisdom, and experience you would need to earn it all back. Knowledge allows you to master success again and again (both personally and professionally) when you develop the skills and the tools to continually win in business. That's what makes success easy!

Shameless, No-Nonsense Action Steps and Affirmation

Success Is Easy Affirmation (say it, believe it, and own it): "Success comes easy to me because I'm a lifelong learner who continues to expand, learn, and grow both personally and professionally."

1. *Remain a lifelong learner.* When you dedicate yourself to lifelong learning, you commit to improving each day, in every

area of life. This includes your level of success, finances, health, and soft skills. These skills help us connect with others and the world around us, not just in business but in our personal relationships, too.

2. *Set a higher standard.* Shift your perspective on what learning truly means. The world is changing every day, and you must commit to lifelong learning to stay ahead and win in business. Expanding your knowledge means diving deeper into your area of expertise. Learning at this level puts you in a positive state of mind and will inspire you to raise your standards and increase your value as an expert.

3. *Commit to expand your area of expertise.* As you learn, you will realize there are more exciting goals to achieve. You will also learn more about yourself and create a greater quality of life, including higher earning power, greater opportunities, and amazing experiences. When you commit to lifelong learning, you are creating a need to constantly improve yourself so you can gain a competitive edge in business.

4. *Cultivate the right mindset.* A lifelong learning mindset requires curiosity about the world and about new challenges, ideas, and experiences. This mindset allows you to create a well-rounded, better version of yourself. It is always open to new possibilities. The only way to reach your success potential is to be open to anything that comes your way and be willing to explore everything. This mindset also allows you to approach life from a place of gratitude, where nothing is taken for granted. Every bit of knowledge you've learned is appreciated and respected because over time it will transform your perspective on life.

5. *Respect the wisdom of others and discover new insights with shared thinking.* The compounding action of shared thinking with successful people moves your knowledge forward faster and easier. Even beyond the immediate need to solve a particular problem, listening to how others approach business or their personal lives can flip a switch in your thinking, leading to a

breakthrough or new insight. When you're excited to learn more, you do more, and work becomes more like play because success is easy!

SUCCESS IS EASY . . .
as You Master the Art of Influence

One of the best ways to increase your exposure and income is to become an influencer. Influencers get others to follow their ideas, which builds success by allowing opportunities to find them.

To become an influencer, spend time and energy creating success in your area of expertise. It's not enough to have a niche—you must *dominate* your niche market. Becoming known as an expert is one of the key components of my success.

The best-known experts are influencers. They offer detailed how-to information that solves problems, offers solutions, and personally supports other people's success. Experts influence others with their knowledge, products, or services along with a systemized, proven result. They may also influence others through coaching or consulting and/or speaking on webinars, video, and live stages. What sets experts apart from others who offer these services is that they specialize in a specific topic or niche market.

What's great about being an expert is that while you are fulfilling your life's mission, you are also influencing and teaching others. As the expert, you can go deeper with your knowledge than the average person in your industry and develop a step-by-step blueprint, program, or system that can be duplicated by other people.

In this chapter, you will discover that influence is about spreading the passion you have for your work. You will also learn that you have an authority figure inside you already—you just need to discover how to bring it out and expand your expert business model.

Do What You Love and You'll Influence the World

You've probably heard the saying, "Do what you love, and the money will follow." I like to rephrase it as, "Do what you love, and you'll influence the world." When you influence others, you are in touch with your passion and can pursue what you love for a living. The monetary rewards will follow the pursuit of greatness.

Having said that, passion certainly helps. Passion gives you the drive and determination you'll need when the road gets rocky or when times get challenging. But you'll need more than that to grow a successful, lucrative business.

You need skills and talent to make a name for yourself as an expert, but passion, skills, and talent alone won't pay the bills. You also need good business sense and an entrepreneurial mindset to make it to the top as an influencer.

Make It Your Mission to Influence Others

We all have a life's mission, a story, a message, or a skill that can help, inspire, and influence others. What matters most is how you share your message. In business, you share it through an innovative brand and a powerful statement that sets you apart from the competition.

The best way to become an influencer is for passion to fuel your desire to be the best at what you know by blazing your own trail. Success comes to those who are willing to stay the course despite adversities, challenges, and distractions.

Influencers are most sought-after for their skills and passion to support the success of others. Influencers don't give up regardless of what mistakes or challenges they need to overcome. In fact, they use mistakes as a way to help shorten the learning curve for others.

My own passion for becoming an influencer came from the many wonderful mentors who shaped my life and career in positive ways. They helped me grow my business and showed me it was easy if I simply followed their lead. In fact, this inspired me to become a mentor myself.

When I launched myself into the expert business decades ago, my mission was to give back through the power of influence. I had no formal training when I started. I had never considered myself an expert at anything before. And if I called myself an expert back then, most people felt I was exaggerating.

To become a successful expert, you must fulfill a purpose others need or want. You must stand out from the crowd and think outside the box. And you must have a shameless desire to do more! Answer these three important questions to see what drives your desire to become an influencer:

1. How will your skills help you solve other people's problems?
2. How can your talents, wisdom, and experiences guide others toward a better personal or professional life?
3. Can you effectively transfer knowledge to others through a systemized process to create learning and benefits?

Once you review your answers, you can start to create a plan that helps you sell yourself as an expert influencer. The first step is claiming that title for yourself.

Claim the Title of "Expert"

The next step is to position yourself as an expert. Why not? One of the definitions of the word "expert" is "skilled person." Everyone is skilled at something.

So what is an expert? According to Merriam-Webster, an expert is described in the following way: "A person with special skills or knowledge representing mastery of a particular subject."

In my experience, an expert is someone who is a touch point for peers and colleagues and can be relied upon to provide advice, wise counsel, and guidance in matters related to their industry. They are people who have extensive knowledge of their respective subject matters by way of education and personal experience, and they may also hold certifications or credentials within their industry as well.

An expert can be believed, by virtue of credential, training, education, profession, publication, or experience, to have special knowledge of a subject beyond that of the average person, sufficient that others may officially (and legally) rely upon the individual's opinion. Historically, an expert was referred to as a sage. The individual was usually a profound thinker distinguished for wisdom and sound judgment.

We all need experts—a wise sage, a super hero, a role model— someone who had a big dream and lived it!

Why not believe in your own dreams so much that you strive to become your own expert, your own super hero, your own wise sage and even a role model for others?

When you step up as an expert, you embrace your own uniqueness by focusing on the marketing skills that can give you a clear direction. You also carve out your expert positioning niche, which allows you to gain a competitive edge over other influencers.

I didn't become an expert overnight. But when I decided to take my business to the next level, it changed the way I did business forever. I love teaching and transferring my knowledge to my clients in a systemized way that helps position them as experts, too. My clients come from diverse industries and backgrounds: business owners, entrepreneurs, coaches, speakers, authors, accountants, nurses, doctors, engineers, financial advisors, real estate agents, and more. Each wants to be seen, known and recognized as the go-to expert within their niche industry. Some are already considered experts; others are simply beginning to step up their game to expert status.

Build a Better Business Model

As my speaking and consulting business grew, it took 100 percent of my personal time and attention to run it. At the time, I was so focused on reaching my goals that I didn't stop to think about how my business income would be affected if I could not personally deliver results.

It's important to create a business that can run itself if, for some reason, the owner cannot be there. So let me ask you this: If you couldn't personally work in your business for a few months, would it affect your income?" If the answer is "yes," consider a new way of looking at your overall business model to allow for time away from day-to-day tasks so you can focus on building your influencer platform.

You don't want a business where income is only generated if you are there to run it. Create what I call a "personal life insurance policy." It's not actually a written policy—it's simply a business model that keeps income flowing into your business without your personal day-to-day involvement.

This is the way to ensure your passion and your business remain alive and well for many years to come. Let me address this in another way: It is risky to always be chasing down new business while you run daily operations by yourself. This business model can set you up for disaster.

For example, what if something—a health issue, family problems, etc.—stopped you from being there to pursue new customers? What would happen then? I don't want to be all gloom and doom here, but life can sometimes get in the way of running a successful business. And that can stop you in your tracks. That's why it's important to generate additional income streams that don't require your personal attention.

Find Additional Revenue Streams Around Your Expertise

There are many ways to pursue your passion and influence others around what you already know without being involved in the day-to-day aspect of your business.

For example, consider the ways that you can create an income stream by influencing others with your knowledge such as public speaking, coaching or consulting, writing, licensing educational programs, online courses, books, etc. All these are based around doing what you love and are brilliant at. Anyone who wants to support others' success can become the go-to industry's expert in their niche to create additional revenue streams. And it might even become their new full-time career like it did for me.

My career change happened after I sold my retail clothing store. I wanted to share my expertise and knowledge of the business with other independent retailers. I was extremely passionate about helping others get a leg up on their competition. I wanted to share the proven success strategies with them that had worked so well for me. I launched my first new income stream as a consultant helping retailers in my area grow their businesses, and next I launched my speaking business. This took me out of the daily business grind of running my

Passions turn into profits when income streams flow easily and consistently to you.

retail stores day to day and brought in additional income. And once I started making good money from it and started to really enjoy it, I decided to sell my last retail store and become a full-time expert. My main goal has always remained the same—to influence, educate, and motivate others to achieve more success that they ever imagined they could achieve.

Learn to Develop Charisma

Influencers create charismatic connections. You've probably met many people you liked instantly but couldn't explain why. It's because these people knew how to make a charismatic connection with you. Charismatic people make others feel good. Charisma is not something you acquire at birth; it's learned.

What is charisma? Can you learn it? Well, all it takes are some slight modifications to your behavior. Charisma is about what you say and do, as opposed to who you are as a person. Intuition, social cues, physical expressions, body language, and the way you treat others all play a part in developing charisma.

Being "present in the moment" is the most important aspect of charisma. The second most important is confidence in your connections. Both show others you are paying complete attention. Without confidence, you may appear like someone who doesn't show interest.

Charismatic people allow you to talk about yourself, which makes them likable. To become more charismatic, you must put others first in a conversation. Shut down your need to do all the talking and don't let your ego get in the way. Start paying attention to the words others share. Invest all your attention on the other person and be in the moment.

To do this effectively, don't just stand there thinking about what you will say next while the other person talks. That may seem proactive, but it shows you're not listening. There's a balancing act to making great connections. You must know when to reply and express yourself in a confident way to keep the talk flowing without taking over the conversation.

One of the easiest ways to form an immediate bond with others is to give a genuine compliment. The key is to remember names. How can you easily remember someone's name? When you're introduced to someone, instantly relate the name to something or someone else. Do it quickly, before you forget. Then keep the mental picture of that other person or thing in mind when returning to remember the name. Research shows that if you use someone's first name at the beginning of a sentence, your chance of influencing that person increases dramatically. This also stops you from using that lame excuse "I can't remember names."

You're Never Too Old to Influence the World

Don't ever walk away from an opportunity by thinking, "I'm too old to take this on." Age should be a distinct asset in any organization because your personal experiences, wise lessons, and good common sense benefit those around you, too. That's when you can be the expert influencer who leaves a mark on the world with a lasting legacy.

Gray hair stands for greater wisdom, experiences, skill, and understanding. Emotional and personal maturity continues to be a tremendous blessing to anyone you inspire. As you get older, you've made more decisions and had more experiences than the average person. This makes you wiser and allows you to guide and support others. No matter what your age, you have much to give back to the world.

When you learn something new every day, despite your age, your mind will be happier, more successful, and more fulfilled.

You Have an Authority Figure Within You

At some point in your life, you begin to realize the only authority figure in your life is within yourself. But before this happens, you look to other authorities and experts to tell you what you're supposed to do.

Deep within everyone's heart is a passionate desire to live a life that truly matters, a life that inspires and influences others in a positive way. All successful people want to make a positive contribution, to

A LIFETIME OF INFLUENCE PAYS OFF

For the past couple of years, I had the honor and privilege of working with the dynamic 89-year-old Anne Lorimor. She is a lifelong learner who continues to inspire others with her thirst for knowledge and her ability to achieve what others believe is nearly impossible. Anne's mission is to help underserved children become all they can be, have options, and receive a hand up in life.

Anne's background explains her particular focus on homeless, foster, and orphaned children. She was born at the beginning of the Great Depression, the oldest of ten children. The family was poor and sometimes cold and hungry. The children wore hand-me-down clothes. For a short time, the family was homeless, living out of a truck with a top like a covered wagon. For a longer period, they lived in a tent on the bare ground, without electricity, running water, or a phone. But Anne remembers people were kind and the family never lost hope.

Anne's family has helped kids for three generations. When an orphanage in which her grandfather had an interest folded, he took in five orphans and raised them with the help of her grandmother and aunt. As a little girl, Anne helped bathe, dress, and feed orphans at a children's home and school her parents founded in rural New Mexico.

Anne became an influencer for change by founding the Challenge Youth Fund in 2004 under the umbrella of Arizona Community Foundation. As her personal mission grew, Anne wanted to help more children. In 2016, she established the nonprofit Lorimor Child Empowerment Foundation, dba Creating Exciting Futures. To raise more funds, Anne needed to influence others into investing in her cause.

Her purpose and passion for helping children drove her to climb up Mount Kilimanjaro in 2015 as the oldest woman to achieve this goal. At the time, she was an 85-year-old great-grandmother. Then, in July of 2019, at the age of 89, Anne set out to repeat the same feat as the oldest person ever to climb Mount Kilimanjaro. Anne set out to repeat the same feat and became the Guinness World Record Holder as the oldest person to ever climb Mount Kilimanjaro. These climbs raised great awareness for her charity, and she became known as an international influencer.

make a difference. Each one wants to live in such a way that the world is better because they were here.

We all should want to leave a positive legacy that lives far beyond us. To do this, you'll want to create more clarity, confidence, and courage for living a successful life that makes a difference in the world.

While writing this book, I realized it had been my mission in life to make a difference for a very long time. I knew my gifts were to inspire and teach others to become more successful. I found my purpose in teaching when I became a professional speaker in 1995. My personal mission became working on being the best I could be so I could bring out the best in others.

Success is about making a difference. It is not found in a selfish pursuit of greatness; it's found in serving others. This means shifting from focusing on your personal success (once it's achieved) to giving back to others in some way.

For example, every time I achieve a new success, I first accept the achievement and feel grateful for it. Next, I find a way to share the success experience with someone else. I thrive on seeing others become successful. In return, success flows back toward me. That's the gift and the power of influence.

Shameless, No-Nonsense Action Steps and Affirmation

Success Is Easy Affirmation (say it, believe it, and own it): "Success comes easy to me because I've mastered the power of influence and position myself as an expert."

1. *Claim the title of expert and step up to a bigger game to win in business.* To become an influencer, spend time and energy creating success in your area of expertise. It's not enough to have a niche; you must *dominate* your niche market. Becoming known as an expert is one of the key components of your success. It doesn't matter where you come from, what your background is, or what level of expertise you possess.

2. *Build a better business model that can run without having to work in the business every day.* You need income streams that don't require your time so that your passion and business can remain alive and well for many years to come. It is risky to chase down new business as you run the daily operations by yourself. Instead, as your business grows and expands, you'll need to create other income streams that don't require you to be there to run the business. This is often referred to as passive income.

3. *Surround yourself with influencers.* Make friends with success-driven people, attend seminars, find mentors, read more books, and watch videos that inspire you to achieve more. We all need positive influencers who will push us outside our comfort zones. This could be a mentor or a friend with a different skill set or different personality from your own. You may find yourself drawn to people just like you, but research shows that capitalizing on diversity requires embracing people's differences. Keep this in mind as you analyze your business circle. Look for people who complement your skills and traits, but also cultivate positive new ones.

4. *Be present during conversations with others.* Invest your attention by focusing on the other person and be in the moment to create charisma. Charismatic people allow others to talk about themselves first during a conversation. Learn to shut down your need to do all the talking, and don't allow your ego to get in the way. Pay closer attention to the words you share with others. Invest all your attention by focusing on the other person and be real in the moment.

5. *Live a life that truly matters by discovering your own internal authority figure.* Create a life that inspires, influences, and gives back to others in a positive and impactful way. At some point in your life, you begin to realize that you have an authority figure within yourself. Before this happens, you may look to other authorities and experts to tell you what to do. Living deep within everyone's heart is a passionate desire to

live a life that truly matters. Decide how you will improve and impact the world with your wisdom, knowledge, and expertise and make a difference by influencing others with your ideas, direction, and guidance.

SUCCESS IS EASY . . .
as You Master in Sales and Marketing

Marketing and selling are often thought of as the same thing, but they are not. The main difference between the two is that the latter requires focusing on what some people consider a bad word—sales—and the former focuses on promoting benefits to fit your prospects' needs. Selling is persuading someone to buy something from you. Marketing is creating conditions under which the buyer is attracted and influenced by your offer to invest in the benefits you provide.

Roles within sales and marketing are changing, but they demand higher-level skills rather than brand-new ones. Retaining and enhancing your marketing and sales skills is critical, especially since effective sales and marketing are a major lever for competitiveness.

In this chapter, you will recognize the need to become a master of both marketing and sales. This requires customer-service and selling skills, not only from yourself, but from everyone who works at your company. You will also discover the top six fears in selling and how to avoid each of them and begin mastering the art of marketing to help you attract more prospects and create more income with ease.

Sales and Marketing Go Hand in Hand

Marketing starts the moment you position yourself, your brand, and your offer. Selling is the logical conclusion to that offer. When a prospect understands your value and buys from you, that completes the process. That's why selling is an integral part of marketing.

These elements work well together when you combine them strategically and effectively. When done skillfully, both sales and marketing help you gain new customers with ease. Both are important to success. Without an offer there are no sales, and without sales there is no success!

In today's customer-driven environment, sales and marketing go hand in hand. Customers have access to a vast amount of information from which to make decisions and sometimes don't even see a sales person until they've already made the decision to buy.

The focus is now on the customer and finding out his or her wants, needs, desires, problems, and pain. And both marketing and sales have the same goal when it comes to this.

Companies with sales and marketing divisions should consider cross training their teams so that they understand how to effectively communicate cohesively together. For example, the marketing management could train the sales team so that they understand the overall processes of the marketing team. The sales management could then train the marketing team to understand their processes. This way the sales and marketing team are both on the same page and can work hand and hand together effectively.

Good Sales People Become Good Marketers

If you love selling, it may require you to do less marketing since you obviously won't have a problem calling prospects, networking, or reaching out to leads. A person with a sales personality is driven by challenge yet has a purpose. This allows them to remain more comfortable speaking up and asking questions.

People with more assertive personalities can persuade prospects to agree with almost anything, get little to no resistance in closing the sale, and quickly overcome the fear of rejection. There are also people who enjoy selling simply because they strongly believe in the product or service. This drives them to shamelessly let everyone know how valuable it is.

A person with a more relaxed or reserved personality may still be able to cope with sales, but feel "forced" to do them. Someone with this personality type may believe sales are intimidating. But everyone can learn how to sell authentically without feeling pushy or intrusive. However, if this type works to master marketing first, they can catch up to the sales process soon after.

Good Marketers Become Good Salespeople

If you love marketing as much as I do, you are also probably a creative sales person. And if you like learning new things, marketing is great because it's always changing and shifting, and there's always a new skill to learn. And it's super fun to see the results—just like selling.

So if you are good at marketing, you are probably a lot better at selling than you think since you are attracting prospects and selling to them even before they decide to buy.

Your clever email campaigns, advertising in print and on social media, web copy, and video marketing could be driving lots of traffic your way. Although marketing starts behind the scenes, it guides the sales process.

Learning to master both sales and marketing is critical for your ongoing success. After mastering marketing, I became a student of sales. I learned innovative ways of selling that felt comfortable, real, and authentic to me. I learned how to sell with an open heart and always from a place of service.

I found a way to make selling fun too. It felt good to influence others and then sell my services with ease. I found people started thanking me for making an offer in such a genuine and thoughtful way. It no longer felt like selling, and I began loving sales. In fact, I learned how to sell so effectively this way that I now love teaching it to others. Selling this way is an art form when it becomes effortless and natural. Selling in such a way that it's truly authentic to your way of doing business and easy for people to say "yes."

> When your head and your heart are aligned, you make genuine strides in sales success!

Master the Influence of Sales

Sales fears are common, but getting over those fears is necessary to succeed in business because you will always have to sell something to survive. Here are the five most common fears in selling and how to avoid each:

1. *Fear of rejection.* Although this is a powerful fear, learn how to get over it, fast. After all, getting rejected by a prospect hasn't killed anyone yet! In sales, the best way to get over the fear of rejection is to understand it's just part of the process. Sales is simply an offer or an opportunity. It's only a challenge when it's done ineffectively, such as when someone is rude, pushy,

or intrusive. But this doesn't happen when you approach sales from a place of service.

2. *Fear of hearing objections.* Many business owners don't have a dedicated sales team, so they need to take on the role themselves. The key is to understand what is stopping a potential client from making the decision to buy, and then not taking it personally. Once you know why the potential client is hesitating, you can reply to that specific objection. When you practice addressing objections in advance, you'll know how to respond to almost anything that comes your way. For example, a client may say, "Your services cost too much." To overcome this objection, justify the cost by breaking down the total investment into smaller pieces so the prospect can see the value and why the price is justified.

3. *Fear of change.* When the market changes, so do sales. Today's buyer is more educated and doesn't want to be "sold to." But the buyer does want to invest in a trusted advisor or a great service. The best way for you to overcome the fear of how sales have changed is to think about a profound impact change has made in another area of your life. This will help you become less fearful of trying something new and help you gain the confidence you need to switch things up.

4. *Fear of talking on the telephone.* Some people are intimidated by picking up the phone and reaching out to prospects. This fear comes from the feeling you are pestering someone. To get past this, avoid cold calling and try to schedule a call time with the prospect first. This de-ices the calling process and allows you to prepare for the call in advance. Asking the prospect the right questions before the call prepares you to get to the point, support your prospect's needs, and make a sale with ease on the phone.

5. *Fear of asking.* Why do some salespeople keep talking about the product or service instead of asking for the sale? This fear puts you in a position where the prospect has to do the work of making a decision. When this happens, there is no offer, and

without a closing offer, there is no sale. If you have overcome all of a prospects, objections and presented a solution in terms that make sense to your prospect, you have achieved your goal and have completely earned there right to ask for the sale with confidence.

Master the Influence of Marketing

Effective marketing is not only the ability to connect, but also the ability to influence—that is, to be a compelling force in the thoughts, opinions, and behavior of others.

The ability to influence others is an art. Although it requires a variety of skills, influencing draws on your ability to understand others and yourself, and that holds true with your marketing as well. Good marketing doesn't have to cost a lot of money. In fact, good marketing can cost nothing at all.

I used to hear this lame excuse of "I have no money for marketing" all the time when I started my speaking career. That's what drove me to write my book *Confessions of Shameless Self-Promoters* in 2005. Even if there is no money for marketing, you still have your talent—market that!

You can learn to promote yourself. And when you don't have money, you need to be shameless about it if you want to pay your bills. When you become an effective marketer, you are also an effective influencer, and when you become an influencer, business and opportunity flow to you with ease. But in the end, it all comes back to a strong, masterful marketing platform. So let's talk about five ways you can master the art of marketing.

1. Discover Your Ideal Client

Customers often think they decide to do business with you. But you must be sure to take on only ideal clients to whom you can deliver the best service and results. In other words, make sure a potential client is a good fit.

When you offer a service, the best way to do this is to ask qualifying questions before agreeing to do business. For example, before I take on a consulting client, I make sure the person is coachable and ready to implement my ideas. If not, we won't succeed, and I would rather invest my time helping a more ideal prospect gain results.

2. Network Strategically

Find the best places to network to gain the best leads, which means getting away from working "in" your business and meeting people at business functions, charity events, volunteering, etc. Getting involved in your community and meeting other professionals who will benefit from your services and/or products is a good strategic marketing move.

When you excel at making influential connections and building stronger business relationships, you will have mastered networking.

3. Market the Business by Sponsoring Events

Be sure to choose the right events to gain the most leads, and turn those leads into warm prospects by sponsoring an industry event or small-business event. Be there as an influencer for your product or service if possible so people can link a face with your business.

4. Gain Referrals from Existing Customers

Referrals are one of the best and lowest-cost marketing sources. When you have a customer who gained value from your service or product, surely they know someone else who can benefit as well. To get more referrals, check in with past and current clients.

Ask for referrals and provide rewards in return. For example, I get referrals from my clients by sending an email explaining the value of offering my services to friends and business associates. I mention how I reward for the referral lead. For example, in one of my personal mentoring programs, I offer my clients a $500 referral fee for anyone they directly refer to me. Once that new client comes on board, I send my client a check in the mail as quickly as possible along with a handwritten note thanking them for their referral.

5. Connect with Prospects Personally

A great way to create influential prospect marketing is with excellent conversation starters. When you make others feel important, your influence goes a long way because everyone wants to feel appreciated, liked, and accepted.

When you fulfill that need in others, you make an impact. For example, when you make connections, ask open-ended questions. When the other person discloses information, it's a result of feeling more connected. You can learn to support your prospects in turn.

Persuading Others Is a Powerful Skill

Ineffective persuasion makes others feel pressured, manipulated, or controlled. When someone uses aggressive, ineffective persuasion, you want to run away! Unskilled persuaders are primarily seeking to serve themselves, not the prospect, which comes across as offensive, rude, intrusive, or even condescending. It feels as if they are talking down to you.

Persuasion is a powerful skill, but many business owners, entrepreneurs, and leaders believe it's hard to master. In fact, it's easy to learn when you break it down into multiple functions. Start by finding common ground with the other person and work on building an emotional connection.

The key to effective persuasion is to highlight the advantages the prospect will enjoy by accepting your idea. To do this, you must first understand the challenges the prospect faces. When you know what's most important to him, you can tailor your conversation around what he desires most and make an emotional connection.

Success requires you to persuade others to buy into your ideas. If you can't convince prospects and employees that your ideas have merit, then the business may fail. The art of persuasion is a critical skill in business.

When you make an emotional connection that persuades, you'll show the prospect that you're emotionally committed to your ideas, services, products, etc. You must show enthusiasm about why it's important to persuade others to your way of thinking. When you can do this, you're practicing effective persuasion that's a win-win for your prospect and you, making you a master marketer and salesperson who can easily achieve success.

Shameless, No-Nonsense Action Steps and Affirmation

Success Is Easy Affirmation (say it, believe it, and own it): "Success comes easy to me because I've mastered sales and marketing skills to gain more customers, more sales, and more income."

1. *Master great marketing skills.* Great marketers are remarkable creators and observers who are open to trying new things and new ways of thinking to get a prospect's attention. When you get good at marketing, sales flow to you with ease. And although marketing starts behind the scenes, it guides the entire sales process.

2. *Overcome the fear of selling and fear of rejection to improve your sales skills.* Sales fears are common. Getting over your fears is necessary to succeed in business because you will always have to sell something to survive. Although the fear of rejection is powerful, you need to get over it. The best way to overcome the fear of rejection is to understand it's just part of the process.

3. *Master selling by learning to overcome objections.* When you practice addressing objections before you make an offer, you'll know how to respond to almost anything. First determine the possible objections facing you; then figure out how to turn them around.

4. *Network strategically.* Find the best places to network to gain the best leads, which means getting away from working "in" your business and getting out to meet people at business functions, charity events, volunteering, etc. Getting involved with your community and meeting other professionals who will benefit from your services and/or products is strategic. When

you become a master at making influential connections, you will also master networking and build stronger business relationships.

5. *Win people over with the power of persuasion.* The key to effective persuasion is to highlight the advantages others enjoy from your ideas. To do this, you must first understand the challenges prospects face. When you know what's most important to your prospects, you can tailor your conversation around those points and make an emotional connection with them. You must persuade others to agree with your ideas if you want to succeed. If you can't convince prospects and employees that your ideas have merit, your business may fail. When you make an emotional connection that persuades, you show prospects that you're committed to their ideas, services, etc. When you can persuade effectively, it's a win/win for the prospect and you, and you'll be well on your way to improving both your sales and marketing skills.

SUCCESS IS EASY . . .
when You Deliver WOW Moments

The key to growing a business is treating customers well. Even if you are not in the service industry, customer service plays a decisive role in the success or failure of a business.

Customers have an expectation of service. They won't put up with rude or indifferent employees, wait in long lines, or accept other bad service for long. Business owners have a great advantage when they discover the loyalty-generating power of exceptional customer support. When you treat customers like VIPs, you stand out from the rest of the competition, which takes customers for granted.

When you understand basic consumer psychology, you discover there are a few behaviors and thought processes typical of all customers. Today's consumers are driven by research. It's easy to research products and services online. By the time a customer is ready to reach out to a business, she may be far along in her research process, especially on higher-priced items like electronics or appliances. To succeed, businesses need to empower customers with information.

Today, customers expect information and services to be available anytime and anywhere. They feel empowered that they are now in control of the buying processs and will constantly demand more, since they actively communicate dissatisfaction when they don't get what they want. But that doesn't mean they don't want you to try and win them over.

Customers control interactions by sharing recommendations and referencing opinions through ratings and reviews. That's why it's more important than ever to WOW them by exceeding expectations in every area of your service and delivery.

In this chapter, you will discover innovative ways to win your customers over and make them loyal (and even shamelessly supportive) fans for life with WOW moments. You will learn why customer service today must go far beyond just satisfying your customers. You'll also learn how to earn referrals, repeat business, and respect from your customers, making it easier for you to become more successful.

Will Customers Respect You in the Morning?

Customers equate their experience with a business's brand. When a customer has one bad experience that remains unresolved, he often writes off that business and heads straight to its competitor.

Negative feedback from customers can spread like wildfire by word-of-mouth—or even worse, on social media. To stay at the top of your game in business, you must look for ways to improve customer service, even if you already think it's good enough. Because good enough is not good enough! You need to give customers more than they expect if you want their respect and love, and if you want them to come back for more.

When I speak at events, I often poll audiences, asking: "Do you give exceptional customer service?" With every audience, the response is the same; the majority believe their service is good. But if that is the case, why does so much bad customer service still exist?

It's because most companies don't know how to deliver better results. Even when I speak to hundreds of franchise business owners who have the same brand and who should be delivering the same customer service, I find they are not delivering the same results.

For example, franchise companies depend on systems and consistency to succeed (as you read in Chapter 14). But sometimes a franchisee doesn't comply with the quality standards set by the company. Some franchise owners fail by assuming they know more than the franchisor, and try to go rogue when it comes to customer service. In other words, one bad apple can spoil the bunch.

To Gain Loyalty, You Need to WOW Your Customers

Customers expect good service, but what if you WOW your customers with exceptional service, which means going above and beyond what they expect? Take the extra steps to make customers feel appreciated. Make each one feel you truly want to give them the best experience ever. This white glove service will keep customers coming back and make them shameless fans for life who will recommend you to more clients.

To create WOW moments, you need to make your customers feel like the most important people in your world. Let them know you will bend over backwards to make their day better. It's all about the overall customer experience—and the details in between. For example, during my client VIP Days, I make it about much more than spending time with me. I create an overall VIP Experience for my clients with great attention to detail. For example, when my personal mentoring clients fly in to Phoenix, Arizona, to have a personal one-on-one VIP day with me, I pick them up at the airport myself. As soon as they arrive, I take them out to dinner, and we start talking about their business. They have my complete attention the entire time they are in town with me from start to finish. After dinner, I drive them to my personal residence where they check into my luxurious guest house where they are my personal VIP guest for two nights.

In the morning they are treated to a gourmet breakfast in our home kitchen that is cooked by my wonderful husband Greg (thank goodness he can cook). After enjoying a relaxing breakfast we start our VIP day in my in-house conference room. We work until lunch on their strategic vision and marketing plan, and then I take them to lunch at a beautiful country club nearby. We have a relaxing working lunch before returning back to my in-house conference room to finish our day.

Our VIP day ends around 6 P.M., and then we go to dinner to eat some more great food (people often complain I feed them too much, but they never turn away the great meals). And the next morning, after leaving them with a few extra surprise gifts, I take them back to the airport to fly back home.

Now, you may not have a guest house or your own conference room to create this type of personalized experience, but there are many ways you can think of going the extra mile and creating an amazing experience your clients won't soon forget and that will leave them wanting to return time and time again. And that's not to mention the great value you will deliver on top of all that experience.

With all the focus and attention that go into launching a business and securing customers, it's a shame not to take care of those customers in the best way possible. This goes far beyond caring, though. Think about the last time you experienced a WOW moment at a business, one where you were really impressed. You probably did a lot more business there and told your friends and business associates about it, too. WOW-ing customers involves creating a memorable, delightful experience to make customers shamelessly loyal for life! WOW every customer by going beyond expectations and providing additional value they don't expect, at no additional cost.

Do What You Say You Will Do, Without Exception

Doing what you say you will do becomes easy when you're dedicated enough to build systems around WOW moments. When your goal is to impress customers, you look for ways to go the extra mile every time. The key is to get your entire team onboard to ensure that they all follow up and meet their deadlines so details don't fall between the cracks.

Giving customers more than they expect can also come in the form of a free gift or more help and support. Everyone loves to get exceptional value. Even little things can create special WOW moments. Everyone loves to feel appreciated!

Admit Mistakes and Fix Problems When Things Go Wrong

Face it, mistakes and problems happen. However, if you don't know how to handle them, they will hit your customer satisfaction, retention, and business success hard.

Nightmare customer service is rampant in the marketplace. We've all experienced it. It's frustrating! In fact, we've encountered so much poor service, we tend to take it for granted at times. That's crazy! Why give money to a company that doesn't care?

Some of the biggest customer-service mistakes include over-promising and under delivering, hiring the wrong people, not empowering and training your team, giving customer policy more importance than the customers, and not asking customers for feedback.

As a consumer, you should not allow this to happen. When I get shockingly bad service, I drive miles out of my way to a competitor. And I will often tell a few friends to avoid the offending business, too. When I discover bad service in large retail chains, I predict that chain will soon close stores or go out of business in the near future.

Bad customer service is usually the result of upper management not instilling the value of good customer service all the way through the team, and managers not being allowed to make executive decisions when things go wrong.

For example, I went to a large beverage big box retailer to buy a specialty beverage. An employee helped me find it and then walked away. I went to the counter to pay, but before it was rung up, the employee asked if I was a store member. I said, "No."

The cashier continued to ring me up, but the total was about $10 more than the price listed on the shelf. When I pointed it out, he told me, "Oh, that's the member price, but you said you're not a member."

I replied, "Well, you never told me if I signed up for a free membership I'd receive a discount."

He said, "Well, we don't always tell people because some people live out of town and don't want to become members." I wanted the discount, if only for this purchase, so I asked him to sign me up.

The employee was visibly annoyed by having to cancel my order and ring it up again, even though there were no other customers waiting. He took my order to the manager and whispered in his ear.

I hate it when someone is talking about me while I'm standing right there trying to do business with them. It's outright rude!

The manager appeared just as annoyed by my request, although he didn't seem busy, either. He canceled the original order, rang up the member price, and handed me a membership card. The entire transaction took only a few minutes.

There was no apology, no "Thank you for your business," not even any eye contact. I threw away my membership card as soon as I left the store. It only took them a few minutes to lose a customer for life, not to mention a few of my friends that I told the story to.

It's clear this problem runs throughout the organization and management. My prediction is this big box retailer will soon meet its demise.

Customer Service Goes Far Beyond Satisfying Customers

As a successful business owner, you should be terrified when you hear about customer service nightmares in your business. But customer service goes far beyond satisfying customers. It's about treating customers well enough that they want to brag about your products and services. It's about making shameless fans who respect you so much it becomes their mission to tell others about the amazing services and products you offer.

Gain Respect from Customers with Feedback

To gain respect from your customers, you need to earn it. Everyone within your organization must be on top of their game at all times to improve the customer's experience. That includes accepting responsibility for your mistakes, regardless of whether it's your fault. Customers prefer businesses that own up to their mistakes and take the necessary steps to correct them.

In fact, customer relationships can often get even stronger when a problem is handled well. To continually improve, look for feedback. Survey your customers on a regular basis and reward them for taking the survey. After all, the feedback supports you and the decisions you make. Customers want to help you improve if you respect their time and value their opinions.

Asking your customers helps you gain a better understanding of your market and the competition. Customers are a great source of information, and they can help you even more when you ask the right questions. For example, ask questions like: "What can we do to serve you better?" Or ask the same question in more detail: "Tell us about the favorite experience you've had with us." Instead of "How is our team doing?" ask "Who on our team made your customer experience special?" or "How did our team create an exceptional experience for you?"

If Customers Are Not a Good Fit: Bless and Release!

On the flip side, you can get customers who are a nightmare to deal with because they lack respect for your value. When this happens, you need to know when to let them walk away. You may even have to fire a client, which is a difficult decision, since your business depends on the income from that client.

Know when to release customers or clients who don't respect you and your team or add value to your business in return. Learn when to break ties and let go. Most business owners find it difficult to let bad customers or clients go. They fear loss of income or suffer from feelings of failure.

A business owner might try to stick it out with a bad client, hoping things will get better. But they rarely do. Even worse, if you have enough troublesome clients, you could end up thinking you deserve to be treated badly. But you need to gather your self-respect and know when to walk away, and sometimes run, from continuing to work with these people.

It's far better to let customers move on than to allow them to treat you or your employees poorly. I had to fire a few customers from my retail stores when my employees began to cringe every time they walked in the door. They became so challenging to work with that nothing my employees did was good enough. They complained about every little detail, causing so much stress it was affecting the service we tried to give our good customers. Bottom line: Don't let your business be held hostage by bad customers or clients.

I've also had to let clients go in my consulting business. I've "blessed and released" those who were either uncoachable or challenging to work with. Only a few would not accept or implement change, and I could tell early on I would be beating my head against the wall trying to turn them around. It is frustrating when clients are not willing to do the work, but no matter how valuable your services are, if they cannot see the long- and short-term value, there's no way to align with it. Again: Bless and release!

Many self-employed people have trouble saying "no" to opportunities that don't serve them well. For example, it can be hard to break free from working with a customer or client who could actually be costing you money, or one who is too demanding. But turning down opportunities allows you to walk away from people who don't treat you and your work with the respect and dignity you deserve. It's hard to say "no" when you need the money, but it will cost you much more in the long run when you agree to work with a customer who is the wrong fit or who takes advantage of your goodwill. You don't have to be everything to everyone. Focus on the top 20 percent of your ideal market to gain the best and most valued customers.

Make It Easy to Gain Testimonials from Great Customers

Don't forget to ask for testimonials after delivering the best service possible. And then make sure to shamelessly use them on all your marketing materials. Testimonials are powerful marketing tools!

Let's say you ask and the customer agrees, but still no testimonial comes. People get busy. So help out and make it easy for them. Write a shameless testimonial and email it to the customer, asking for permission to use it. In the email, be sure to mention that you understand how busy she is and that you are writing the testimonial based on comments she has made to you, which may help get the testimonial done. Ask the client to either use the one you wrote or adjust it to fit. I've received some of my best testimonials this way. Most of the time, my clients use my exact wording and then add even more great comments. Shameless? Yes! Effective? Also yes!

Always Follow Up and Follow Through

Follow-up and follow-through are two strategies most businesses tend to ignore. Many businesses spend a lot of time, money, and effort chasing down new customers, only to lose them after the first or second transaction because they don't follow up or follow through after the sale. If customers don't feel appreciated, they are likely to go to your competitors instead of making you their choice for repeat business.

Following up with existing customers is where the money is! When customers have had good experiences doing business with you, it's a heck of a lot easier to get repeat business than to chase after new leads. Customers are burned so many times by bad service it's a shock when companies have good follow-up and follow-through. That seems crazy, but it's true! When someone follows up, you want to stick with the business and refer it to others.

For example, I recently purchased a beautiful custom-made wooden desk and cabinet for my office. I would give my shopping and service experience five stars from the start all the way through the delivery. But then it stopped!

Since the service was so good during my purchase and delivery, I was shocked that it did not continue with at least a follow-up call, email, or handwritten note to ensure I was satisfied with my new purchase. But nothing came. Crickets!

Although I was happy with my purchase and didn't have any problems, I wanted a follow-up as a gesture of appreciation. After all, it was very expensive furniture, and I felt I should get at least a "thank you." Nothing happened. I've made other high-end purchases and never received a follow-up then, either. This continues to shock me!

The lesson: Always give customers more than they expect, especially after the purchase to show your appreciation for their business. Following up makes customers feel special and gives them a chance to be heard and engage effectively. Existing customers who receive a follow-up are more likely to purchase more products or services. So make follow-up and follow-through a consistent mission. Train everyone on the team to think and feel the power of the follow-up and follow-through with every customer, every day, every time.

Follow-Up and Follow-Through Strengthens Connections

It's easy to think of follow-up just as sending thank-you notes and connecting by email. These are important, but you should also follow up in a way that customers least expect. A personal touch goes a long way toward building lasting business relationships and creates a WOW element of surprise that serves your customer and your company.

When you pick up the phone and ask customers how your product or service is working, just for the sake of doing it, it has two distinct benefits. First, it lets you connect with a customer to see if there are any problems you need to solve. Second, if everything is great, the customer still has the satisfaction of knowing you care.

Most people are not good at following up. Some people come across as too pushy, and others are too passive. Therefore you can stand out by honing this important skill.

To get good at follow-up, you need to practice, which mostly involves creating the process and improving the habit. Most people think of following up as a system to make sure everything gets done, but that's only part of it. Follow-up is what you do to ensure you build the strongest, longest-lasting relationships possible. Think of each new customer as a lifetime customer, no matter the size of the sale. Consider how to build customer relationships beyond the initial sale. Your enthusiasm determines your success. Combine this with the benefits you offer to customers and take the most effective steps to follow up and follow through.

Shameless, No-Nonsense Action Steps and Affirmation

Success Is Easy Affirmation (say it, believe it, and own it): "Success comes easy to me because I always deliver more than my customers expect with WOW moments and personalized experiences."

1. *Treat customers like VIPs.* Customer service plays a decisive role in the success or failure of a business. When you deliver more than customers expect, you stand out from your competitors, who may take their customers for granted. Negative feedback from customers can spread like wildfire from word-of-mouth—or even worse, on social media. To remain at the top of your game in business, look for ways to improve customer service, even if you already think it's good enough. Good enough is not always good enough!

2. *Learn how to WOW your customers.* Begin to WOW your customers with exceptional service by going far beyond what they expect. Take the extra steps to make them feel appreci-

ated. Make each person feel that you truly want to provide the best experience ever. Let your customers feel like the most important people in your world, and let them know you will bend over backwards to make their day better. It's all about the overall customer experience and the details in between. This kind of service keeps customers coming back and makes them shameless fans of your business for life.

3. *Always do what you say you will do, without exception.* Admit mistakes and fix problems quickly when things go wrong. Follow up with existing customers—that's where the money is! When customers have had good experiences doing business with us, it's a heck of a lot easier to get repeat business than chase after new leads. Therefore, treat your customers right from the start and continue to deliver your best efforts every time.

4. *Earn respect from your customers and turn them into shameless fans.* Everyone within your organization must be on top of their game at all times to improve customer service. With all the focus and effort that goes into launching a business and securing customers, it's a shame not to take care of those customers in the best way possible. This goes far beyond just caring, though. Think about the last time you had an amazing customer service moment. You probably continued to do business with that company and may have even told your friends about the experience. WOW-ing customers involves creating a memorable, delightful experience that goes far beyond expectations by providing additional unexpected value.

5. *Make follow-up and follow-through a consistent mission.* This makes it easy for customers to continue doing business with you, instead of your competitors. Always give customers more than they expect, especially after the purchase, to show your appreciation for their business. Follow-up makes customers feel special and gives them a chance to be heard and engage effectively. Existing customers who receive follow-up are more likely to purchase more products or services.

The Final Word: Be Brave Enough to Define Your Own Success

We've tackled the concept of success by exploring ways to master your business at many levels. See? I told you it could be easy! And now, as we close out our time together, I want to leave you with some final thoughts.

First, listen to who you are at your core when it comes to defining a vision you are proud of. It is the best guidance you can get. Following it is where your success really lies. This is the most precious contribution you can make to yourself and others. When you are truly yourself, you will naturally ease into the best possible role in business, and that will be reflected in how you treat your customers. Create your own definition of success, and it will become fun and easy. And when that fun and easy feeling starts to fade, it's time to reinvent and define yourself all over again.

Create your own rules for success and play the game to win. To keep growing for the rest of your life, the ability to create your own rules is perhaps one of the greatest skills and personal pleasures you can have.

As a conscious reflection of your own values, personal rules create a ripple effect on your behaviors and interactions with others. This allows you to create your own unique vibrations or energy. You can see a ripple effect in action when you throw a pebble into a pond. A circle forms in the water, and then another and another, rippling outward and expanding. That vibration happens in business and in life when you are willing to expand, grow, and change. Each vibration creates more and more movement. Each success leads to more success with ease.

additional success resources

Want more ongoing, next-level, and personalized training? Here are some success resources to help you thrive!

FREE *Success Is Easy* Video Training Tips and motivational quote images at www.DebbieAllen.com

Join Debbie's Success Is Easy online training course:
http://www.successiseasybook.com/

Book Debbie Allen to speak at your next event:
Corporate office based in Phoenix, AZ:
phone: 480-634-7691
website: www.DebbieAllen.com

To learn more about Debbie Allen's business consulting and articles
with Entrepreneur.com go to:
https://www.entrepreneur.com/author/debbie-allen

Join Debbie Allen's Success Is Easy Facebook Group for Free
Resources and Ongoing Motivation:
https://www.facebook.com/groups/successiseasy123/

Follow Debbie Allen on social media:
YouTube: www.SuccessIsEasy.tv
https://www.facebook.com/DebbieAllenInternational/
https://www.pinterest.com/debbieallencsp/
https://twitter.com/debbieallencsp
https://www.linkedin.com/in/debbieallenspeaker/
https://www.instagram.com/debbieallen.csp/

acknowledgments

When I started writing this book, I had no idea how my ability to remain strategic in my own business was going to be tested. Just coming up with the final title for the book took me an entire year. I guess that part was not as "easy" as it first appeared.

As I began, my laser-focused attention was on success every day and everywhere. I believed if everyone thought about success more often, more successful people would exist. I paid close attention to the words, meanings, and feelings my friends, family, and business associates used when describing success.

I thank all of them for their open and candid responses in support of the book's concept—and for their patience in listening to my incessant chatter and obsession with the topic of success.

I discovered that everyone's feelings about success are different, whether it's a feeling of happiness, wealth, freedom, or achievement. Almost everyone I talked to said success was one of the best feelings they ever experienced. I learned about people enjoying the tangible benefits of success, such as monetary gain and recognition. But more important was how each one was enjoying the personal growth that allowed them to stretch and learn. I also discovered the different meanings of success at different times in each person's life.

I would love to thank my wonderful husband, Greg, for being my biggest fan and for supporting me in the success of this book. I'm blessed that Greg is always by my side, ready to jump in and support me every step of the way in both my business and my life.

I'm forever grateful for my friend and business associate Jeffrey Hayzlett, celebrity speaker and host of *C-Suite with Jeffrey Hayzlett*, for introducing me to my dream publisher, Entrepreneur Press.

A huge thank you goes out to the amazing team at Entrepreneur Press, including Vanessa, Danielle, Jen, and Kathy for their enthusiasm and support of this book project. And Karen from Eliot House Productions for helping me wrap up the project to the end. The positive commitment to publishing this book happened so quickly, it appeared almost surreal. Or is it simply that success really is that easy?

Another big thank you goes out to The Book Writing Business Coach, Arlene Gale, for her ongoing commitment to this book project for more than two years. She didn't just handle the project with professionalism; she made working on it fun.

I still laugh inside when I think of how Arlene buried me in Post-it® notes during our first full brainstorming day together. And I must say that I now have a newfound respect for Post-its®!

It would have been an enormous challenge to complete such a huge book project without the support of my great clients, whom I thank for their continued trust in my business mentorship. It's an honor to see the success and growth in their businesses happen so quickly, right before my eyes.

I also want to thank everyone who has taught me along my journey and showed me just how easy success could be with their wisdom, guidance, and support.

Plus, one last thanks to my readers for investing in this book. Read through its pages and keep a highlighter in hand to capture the "Shameless, No-Nonsense Action Steps and Affirmations" of advice that speak directly to you. I honor and respect your ongoing commitment to success!

about the author

Debbie Allen has been able to achieve success easily with any business she set her mind to since becoming an entrepreneur at the young age of 19. Since then, she has built and sold numerous million-dollar companies in diverse industries. Her extensive business-building wisdom and entrepreneurial insight has allowed her to overcome countless business obstacles and challenges along her journey.

She is an award-winning entrepreneur and the recipient of the Blue Chip Enterprise Award, presented by the National Chamber of Commerce for overcoming business obstacles and achieving fast business growth. After building and selling multiple businesses, Debbie started her professional speaking and business consulting company in 1997, which focuses on helping business owners and entrepreneurs create fast growth. Since starting her speaking and writing career, Debbie has inspired and educated thousands of people around the world.

Debbie is a bestselling author of nine books, including *Confessions of Shameless Self Promoters*, *Skyrocketing Sales!*, *The Highly Paid Expert*, and *Success Is Easy*.

Debbie also hosts her own live events, bringing business owners and entrepreneurs to her workshops, specialty events, and online training each year. She is known and respected worldwide as one of the top marketing and business growth experts. She is a highly sought-after motivational business speaker who has achieved success as a CSP (Certified Speaking Professional) by the National Speakers Association. She has presented before thousands of people in 28 countries around the world.

Learn more about Debbie Allen's *Success Is Easy* podcast, training courses, professional speaking topics, business mentoring, and live events at https://debbieallen.com and and SuccessIsEasybook.com.

index